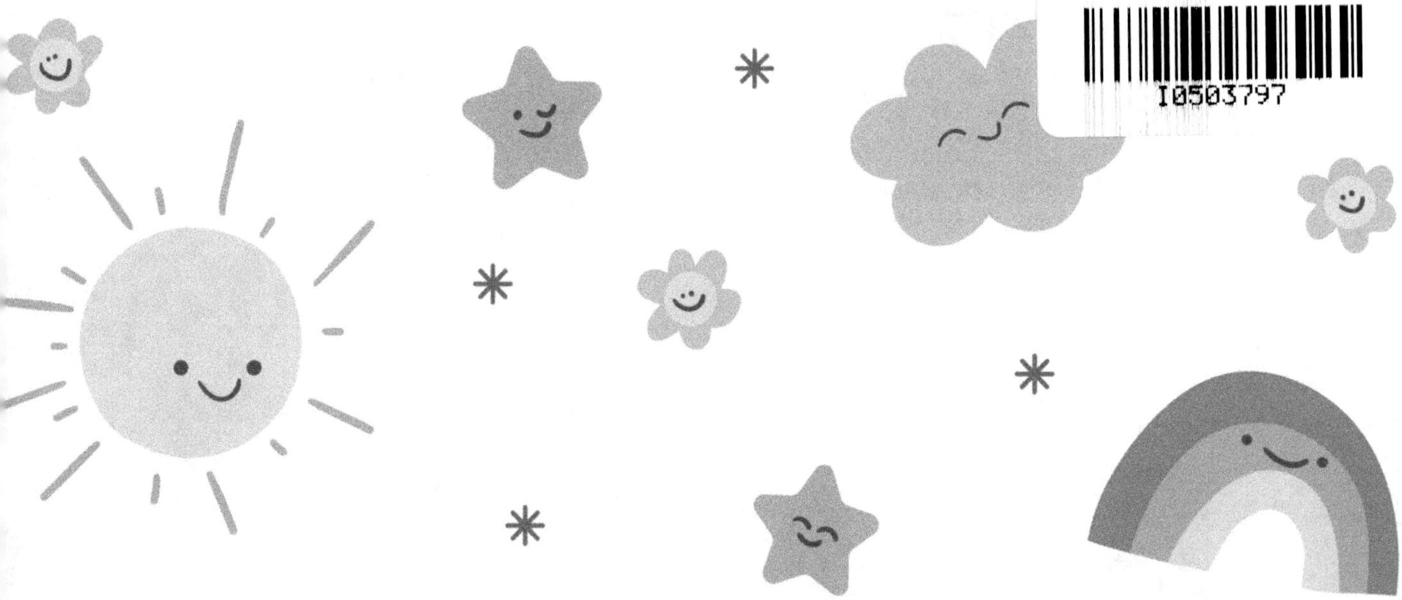

This Books Belongs To.........

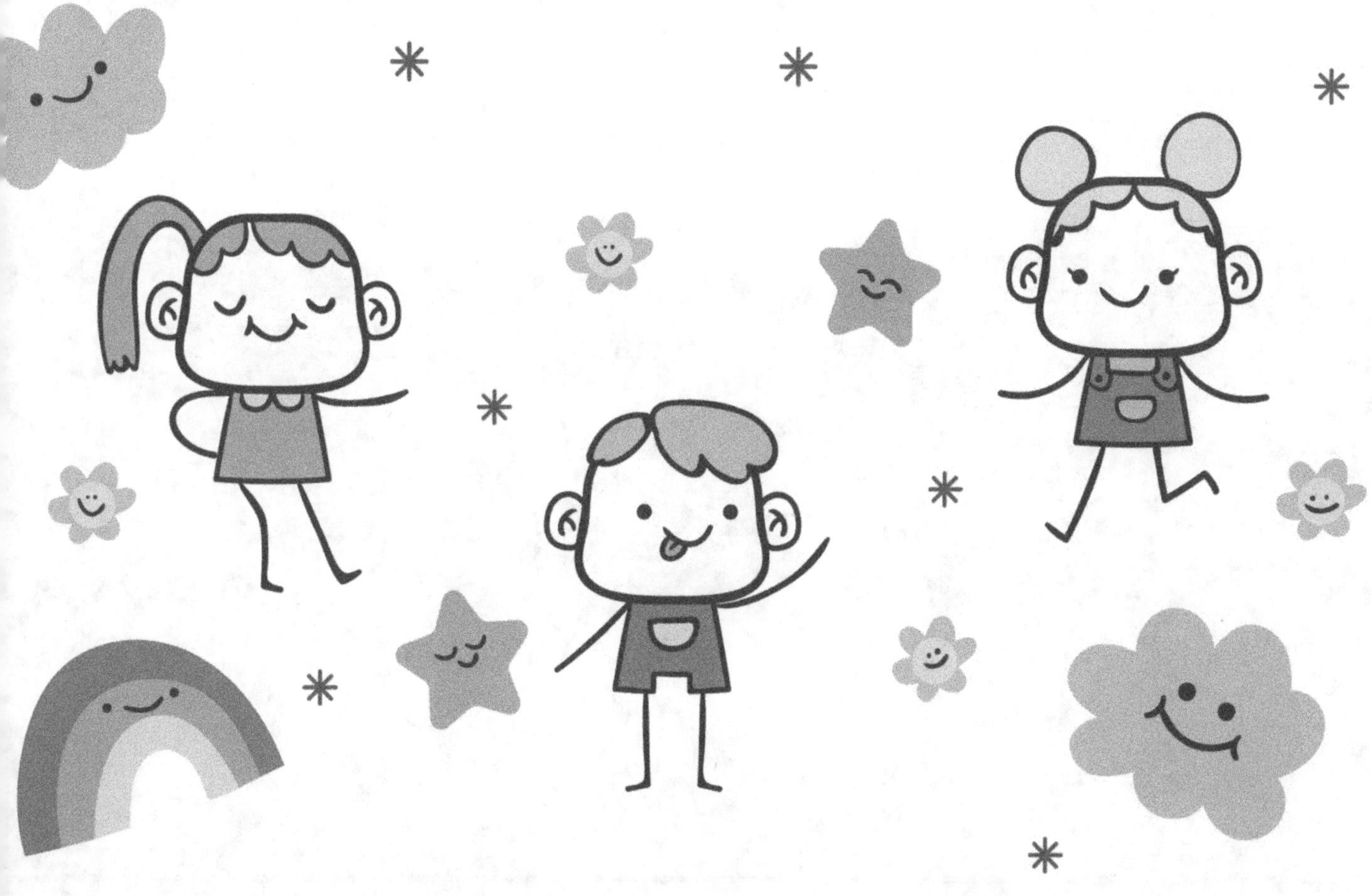

....

....

....

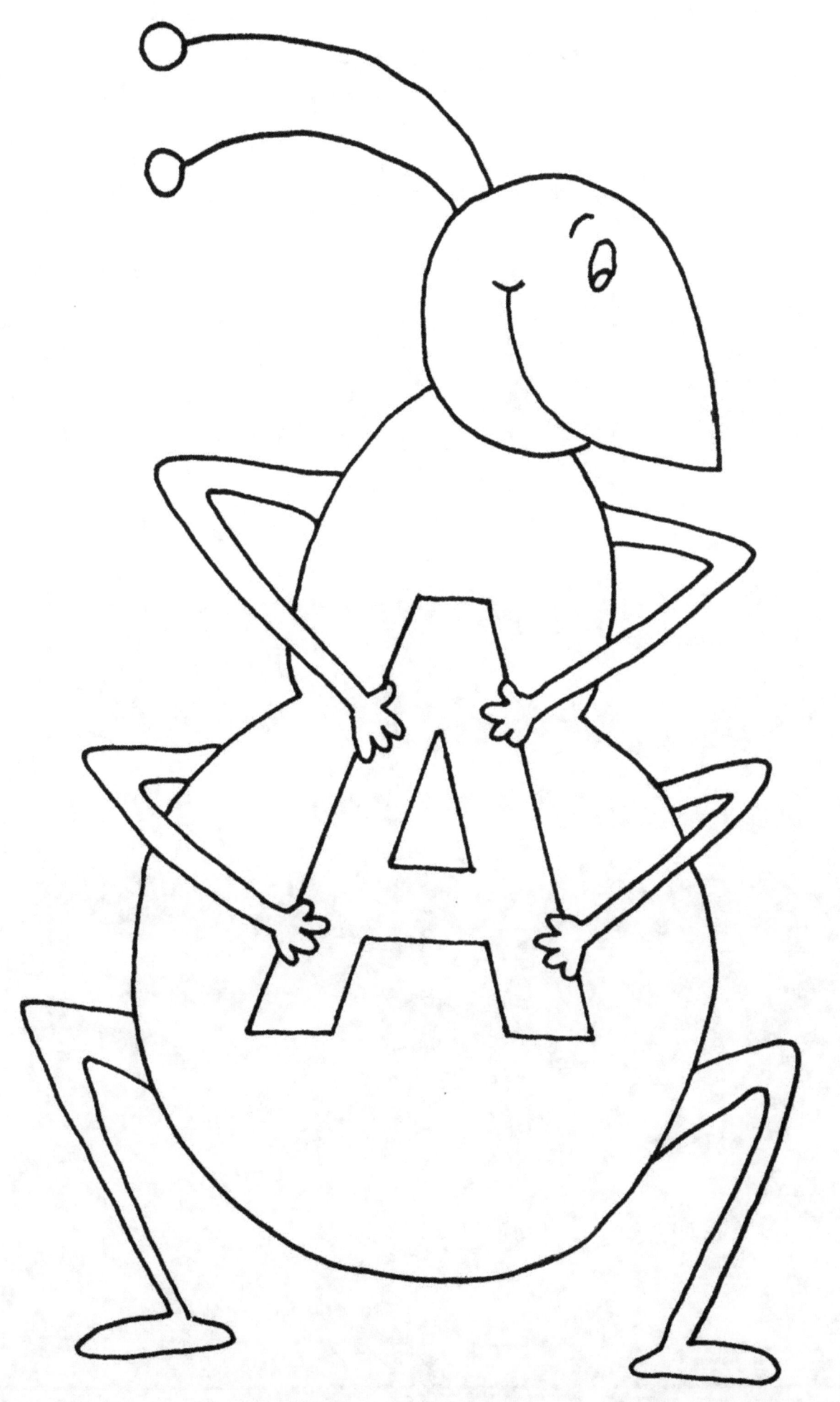

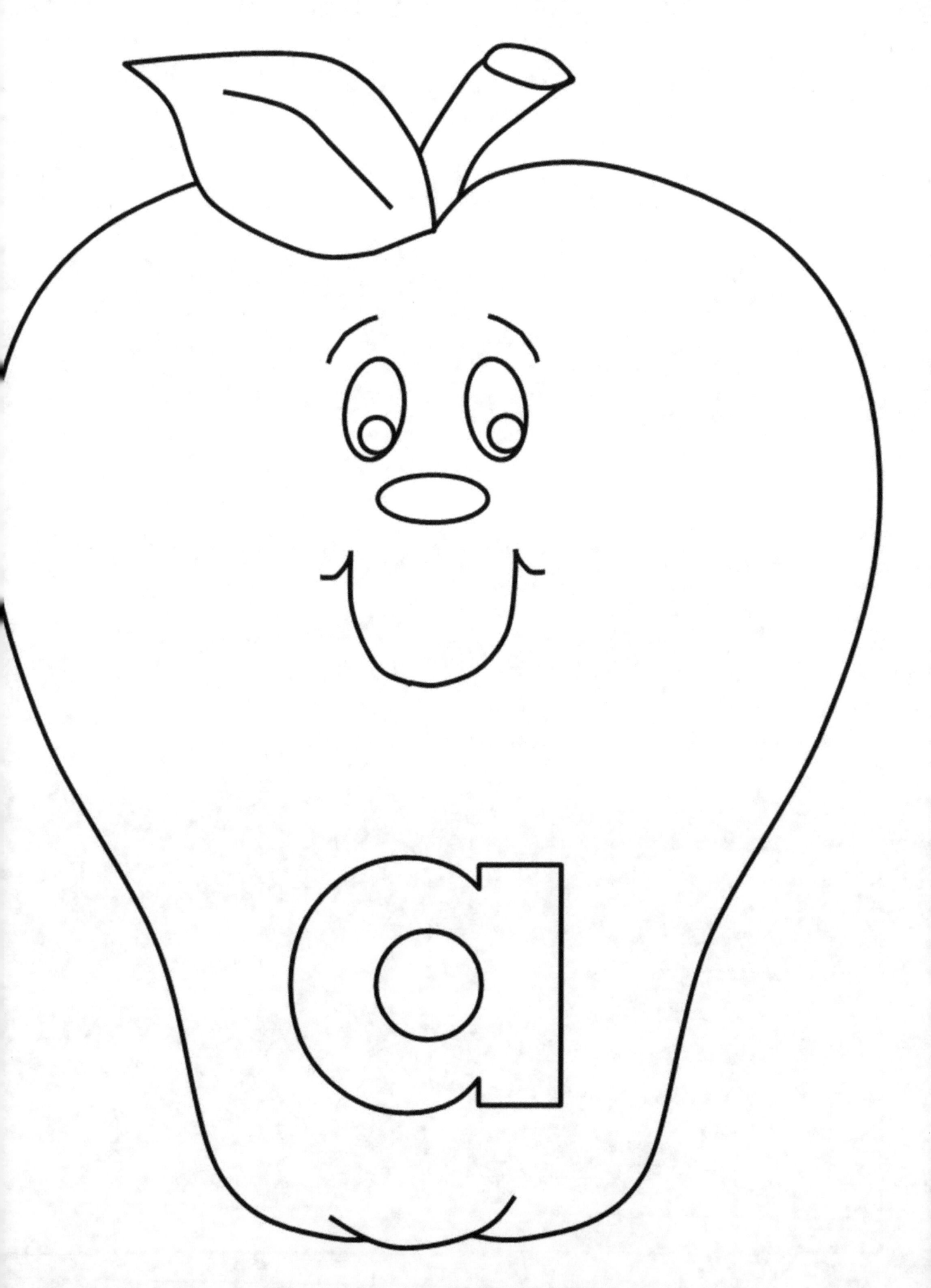

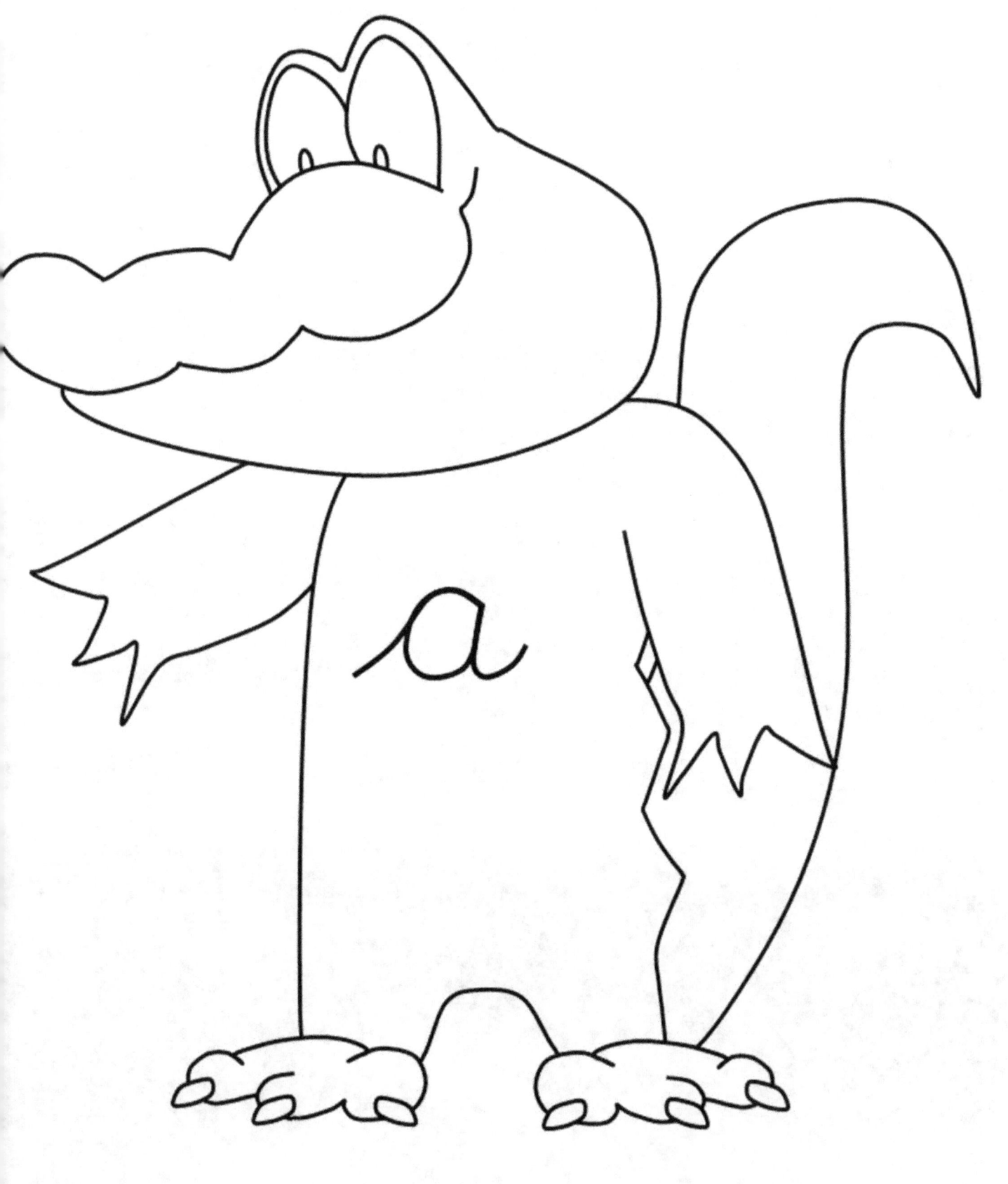

Trace the steps for making the letter a on the following line.

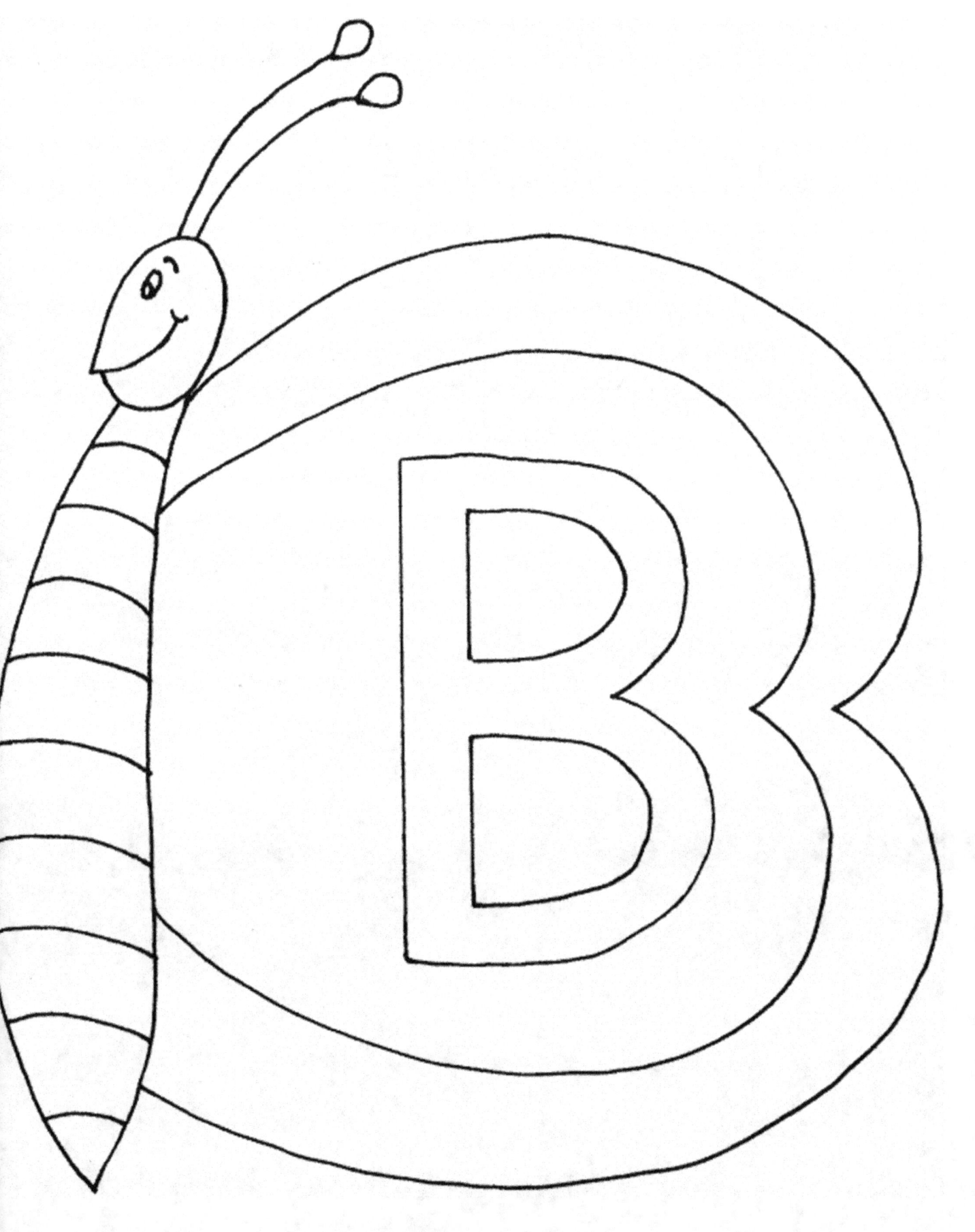

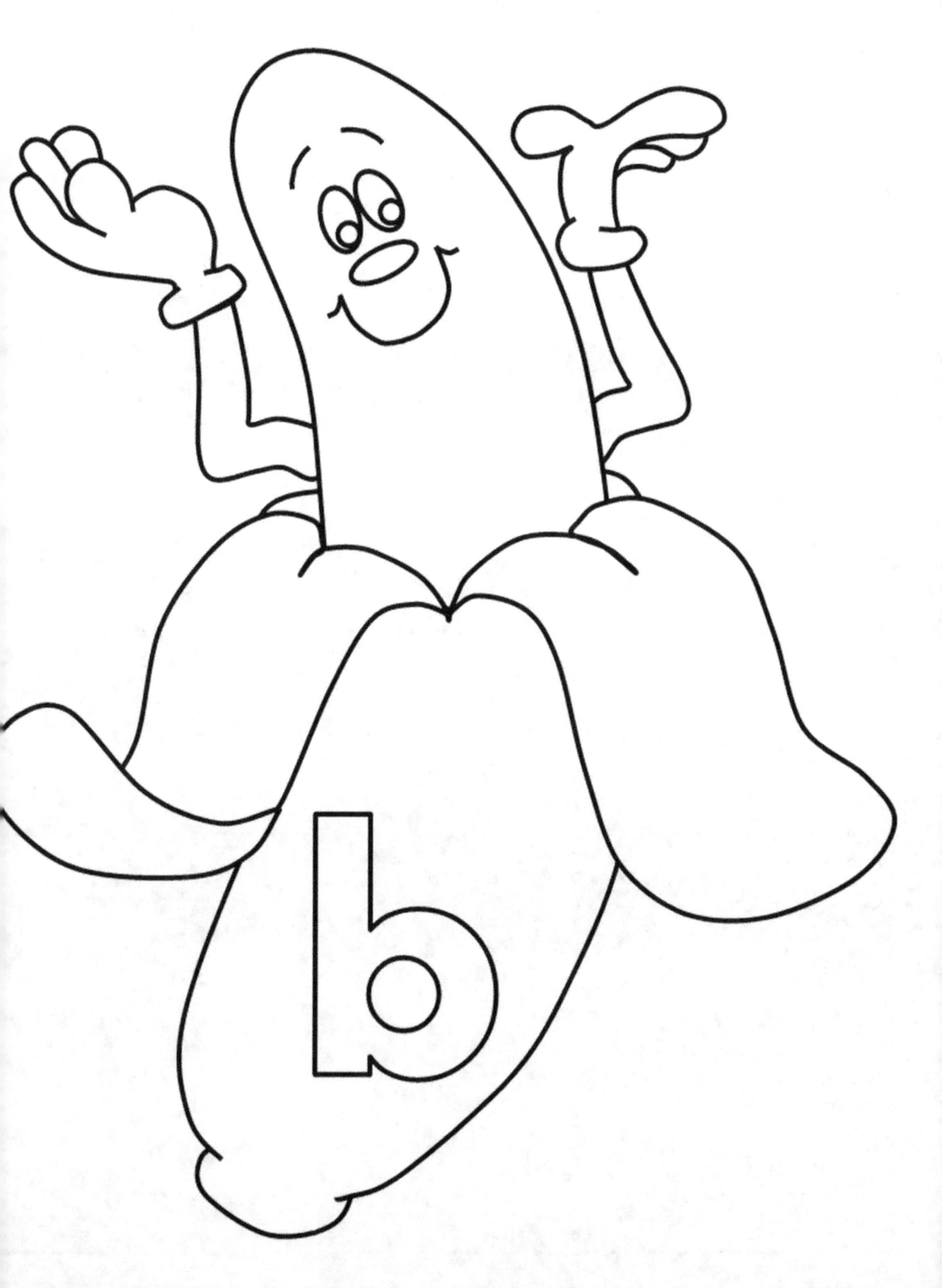

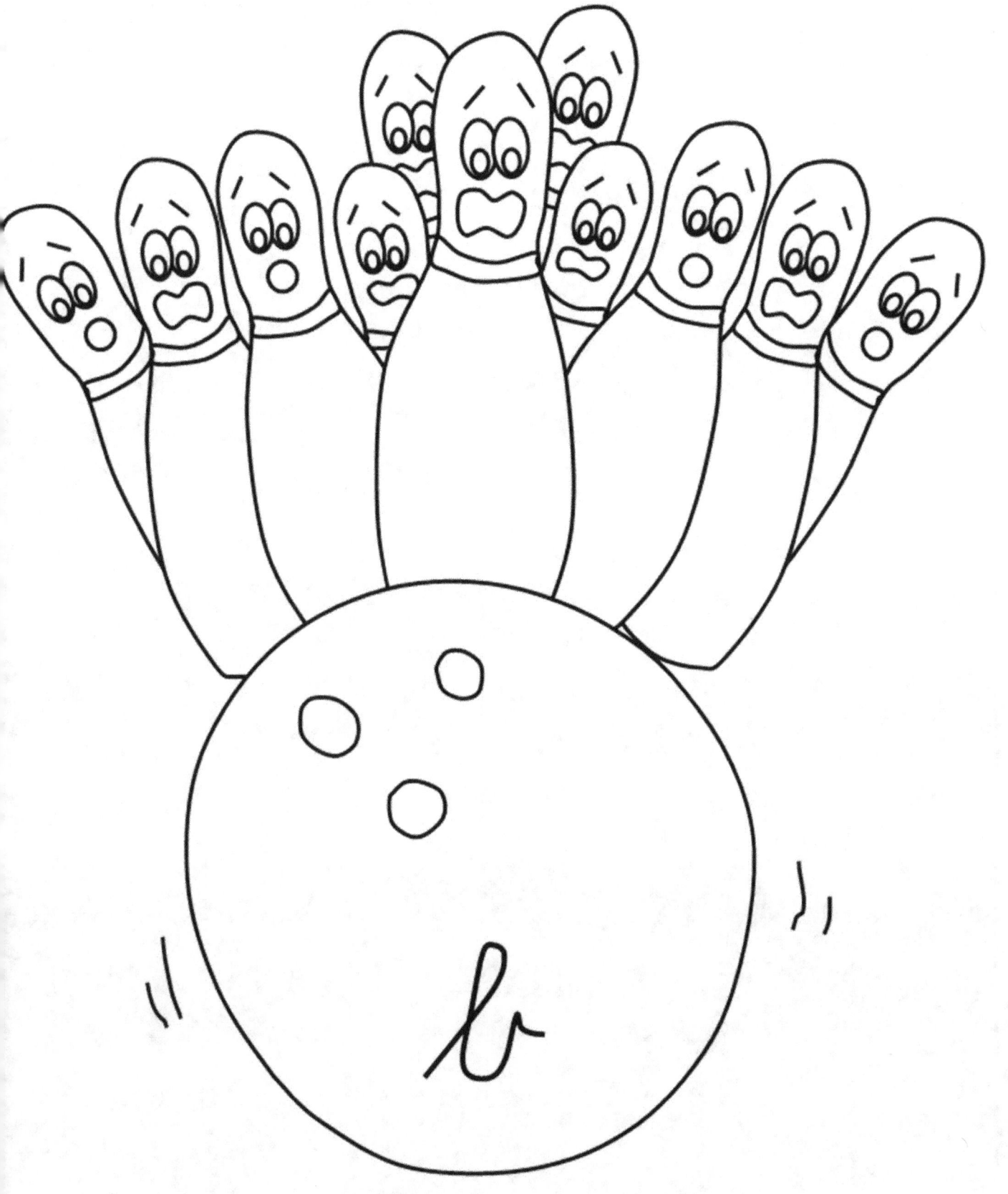

Trace the steps for making the letter b on the following line.

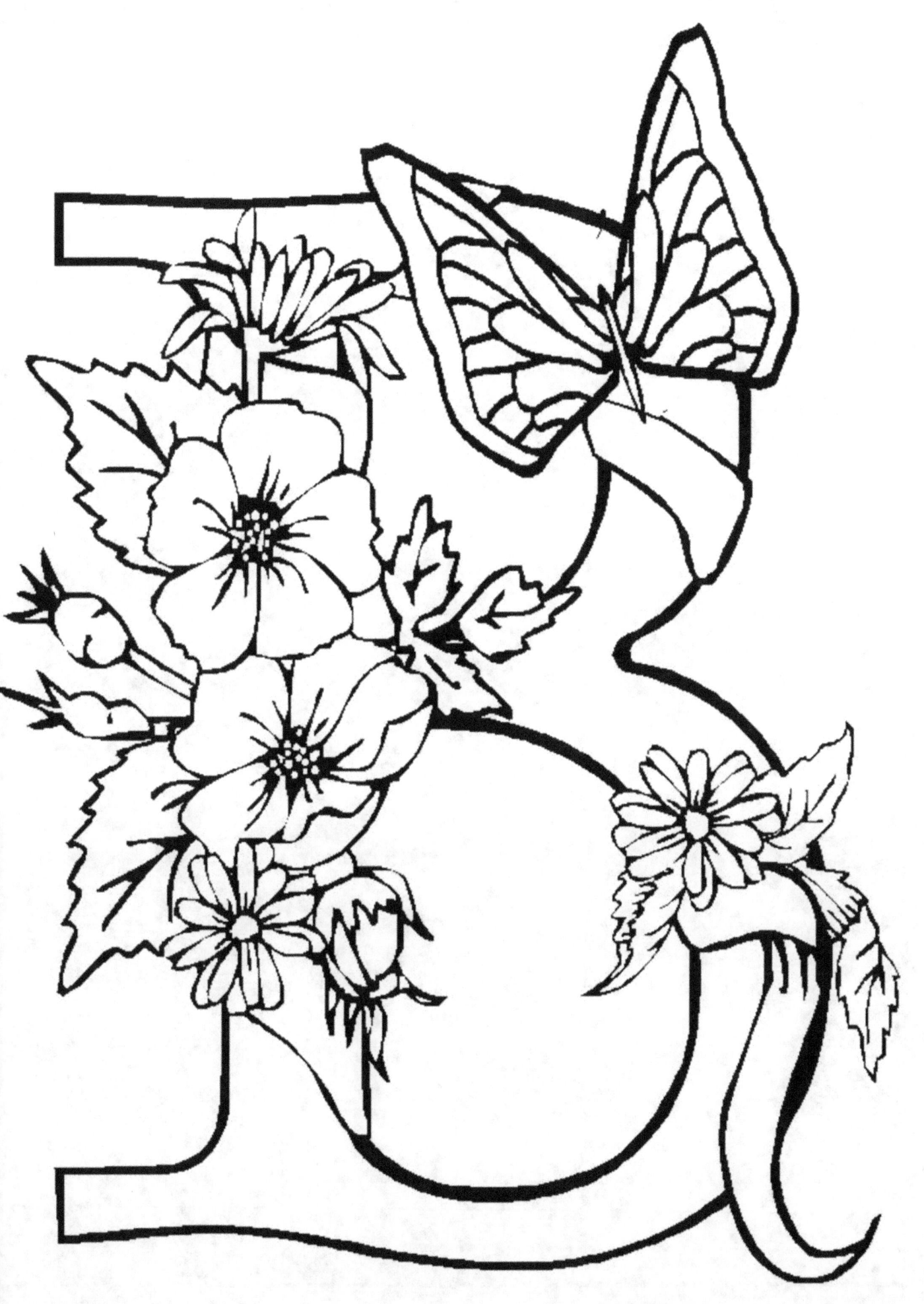

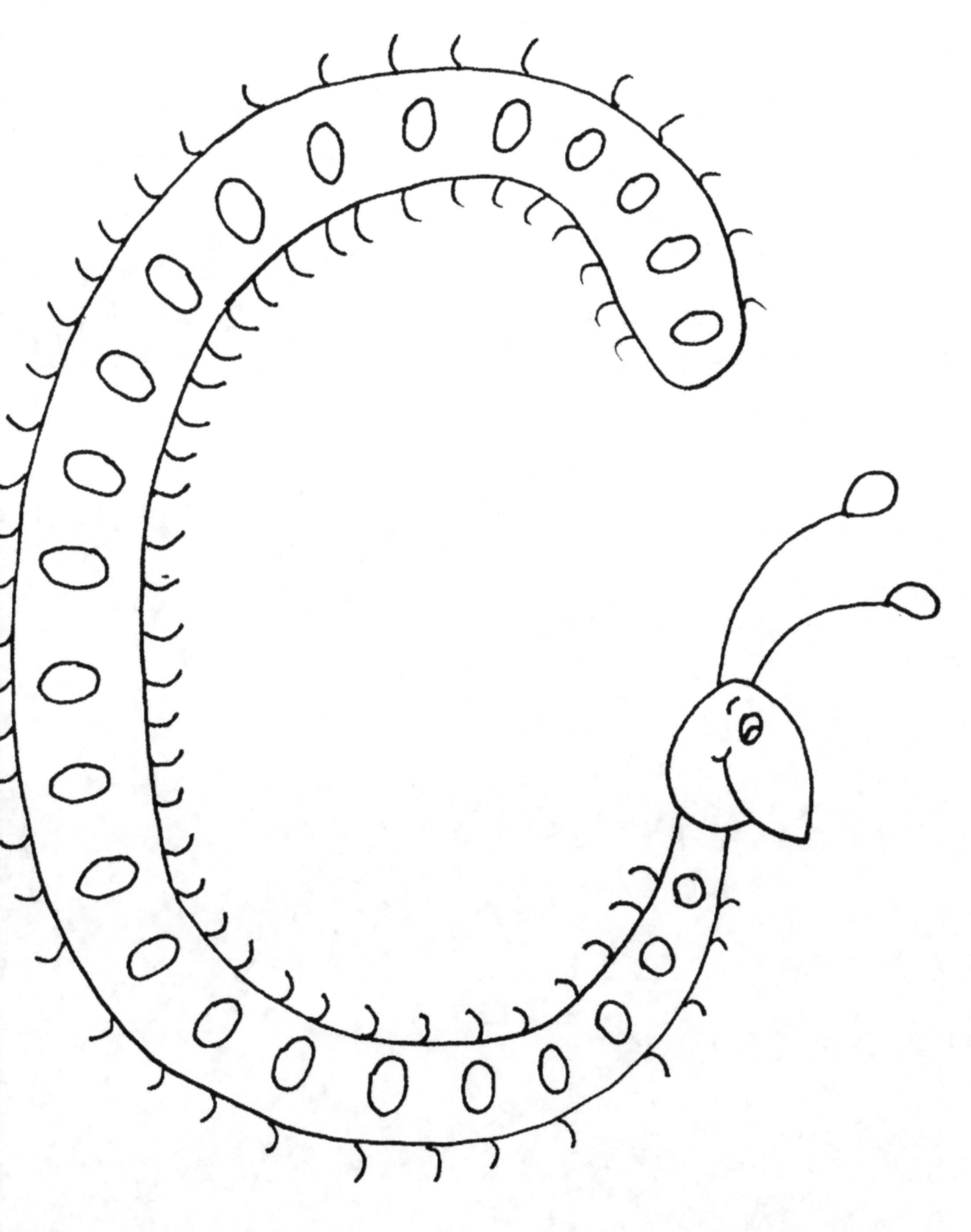

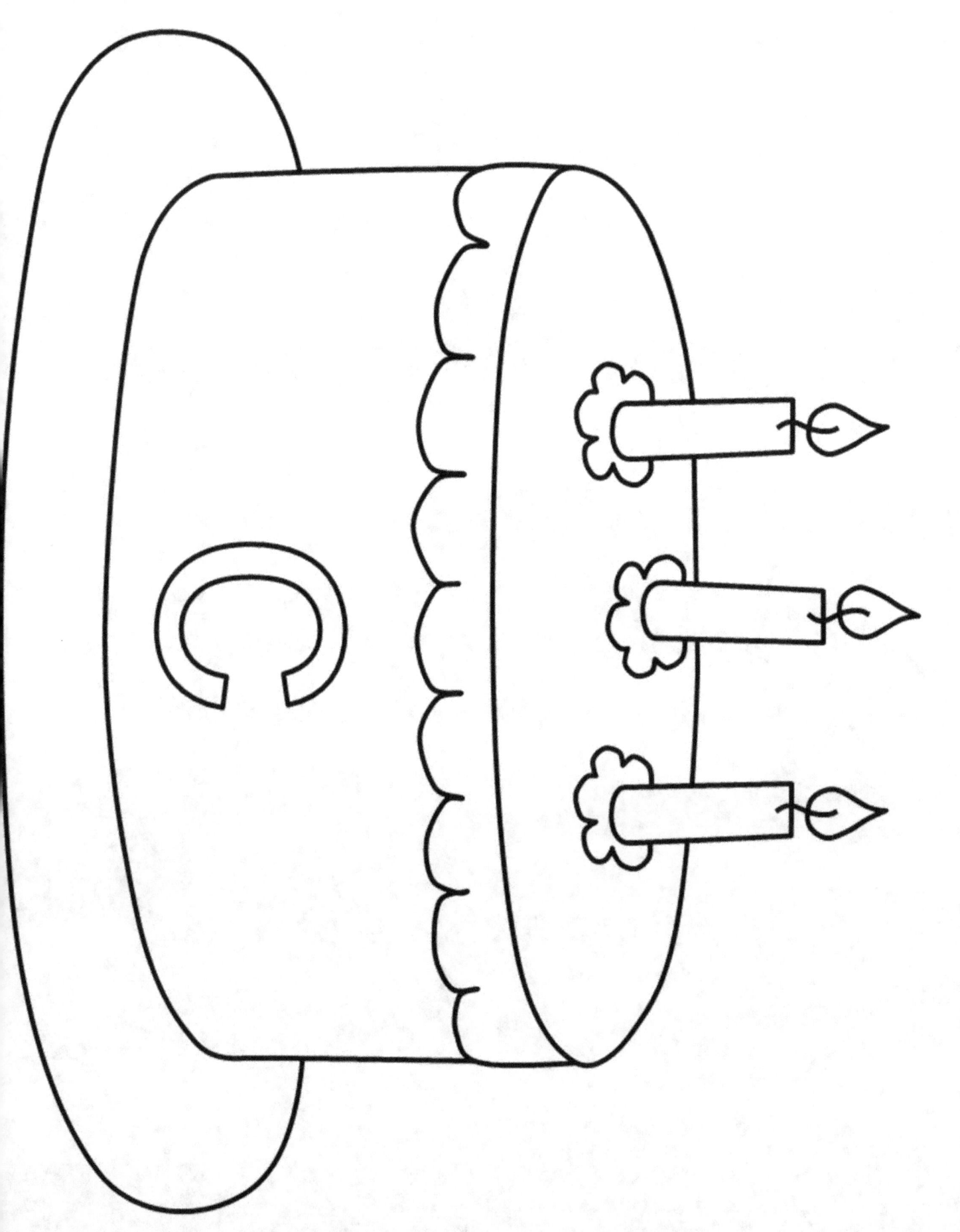

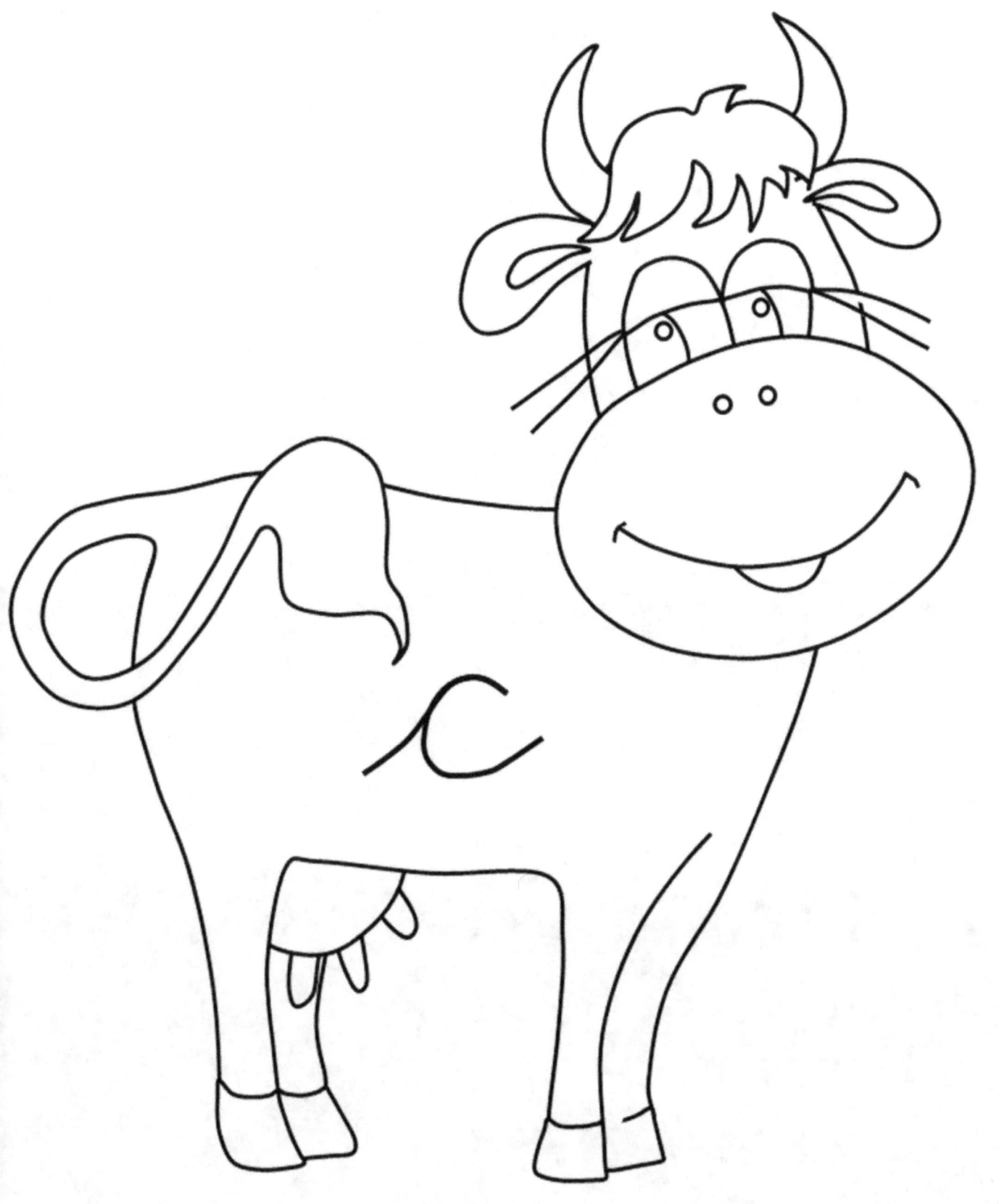

Trace the steps for making the letter c on the following line.

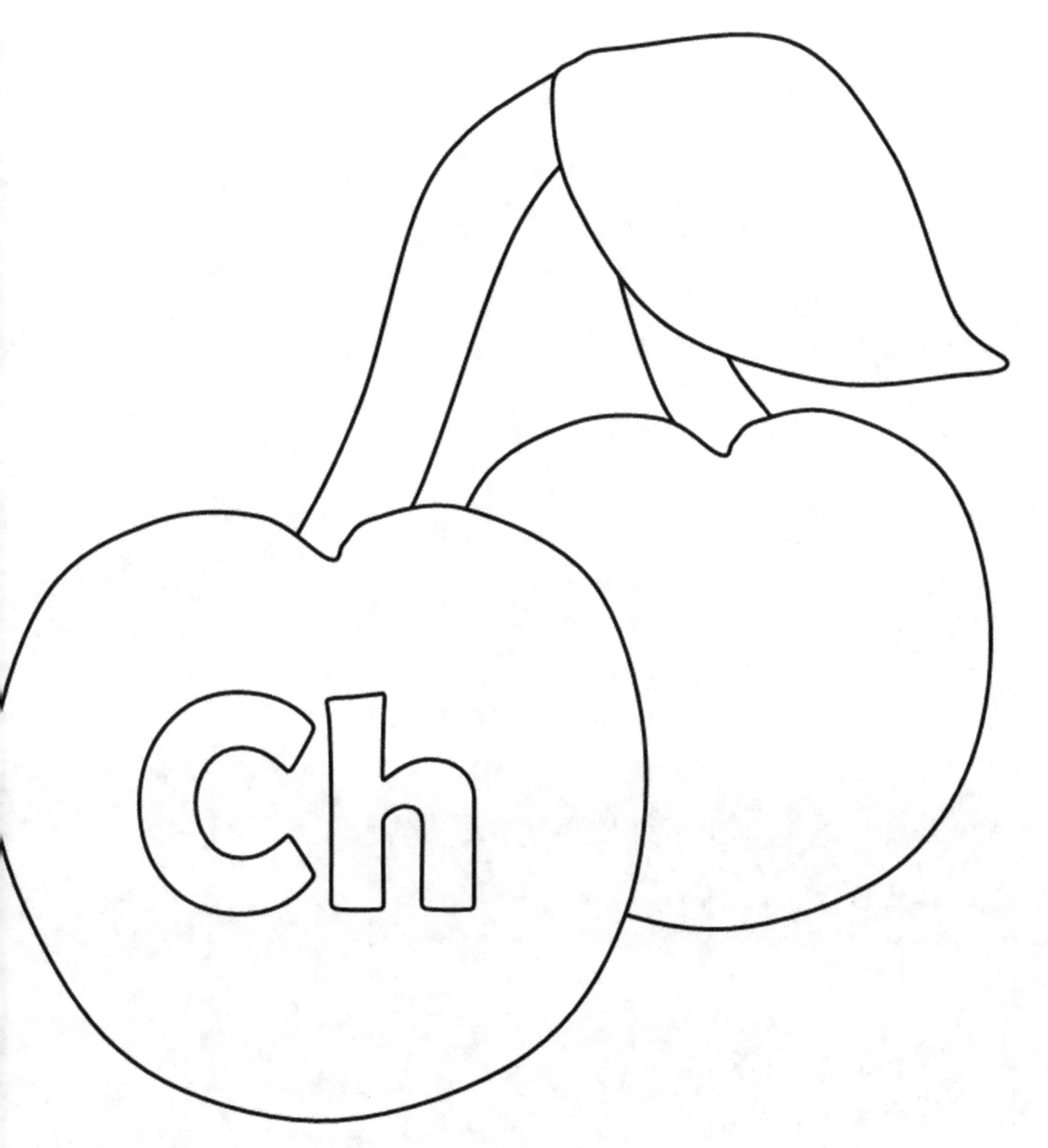

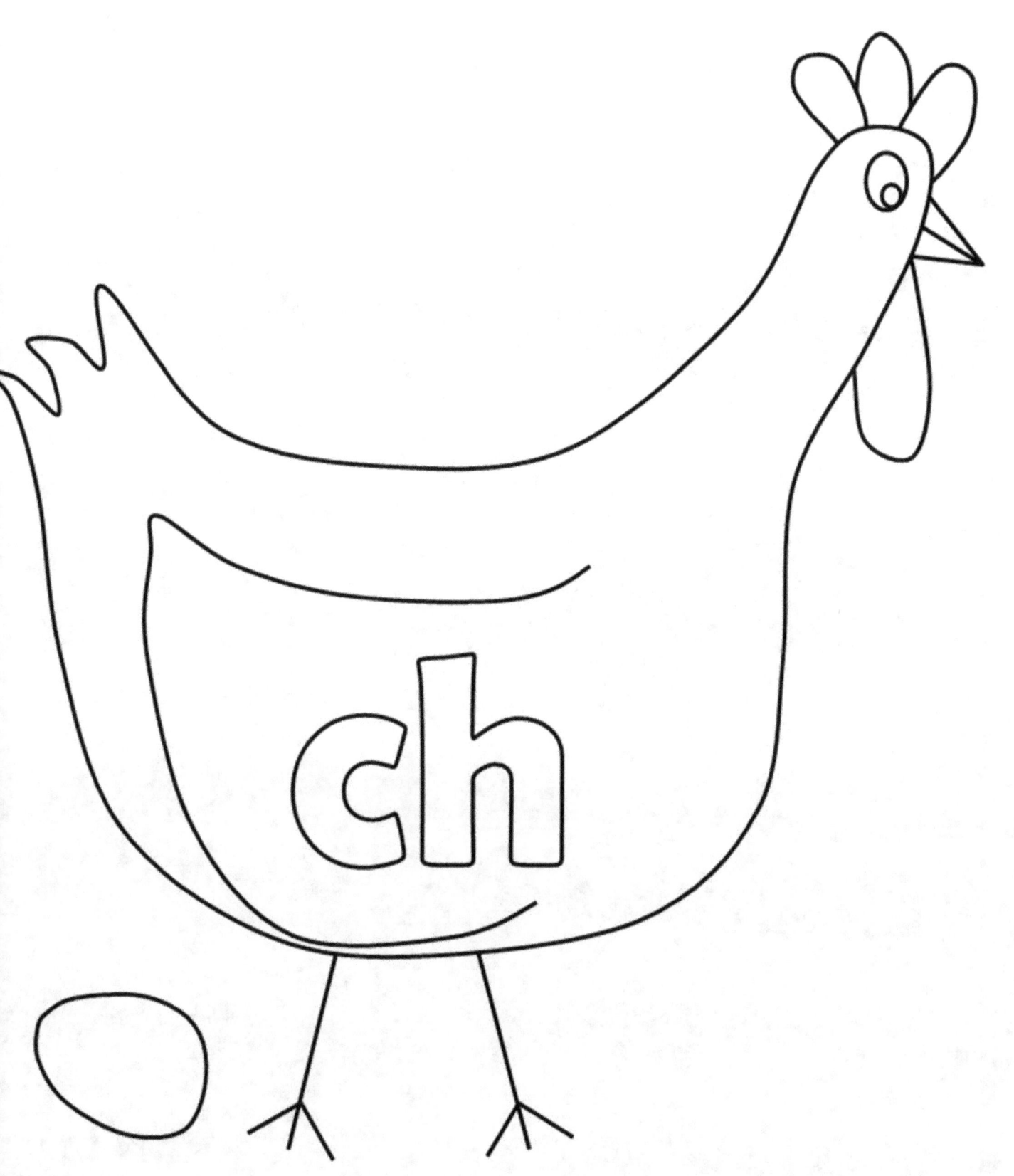

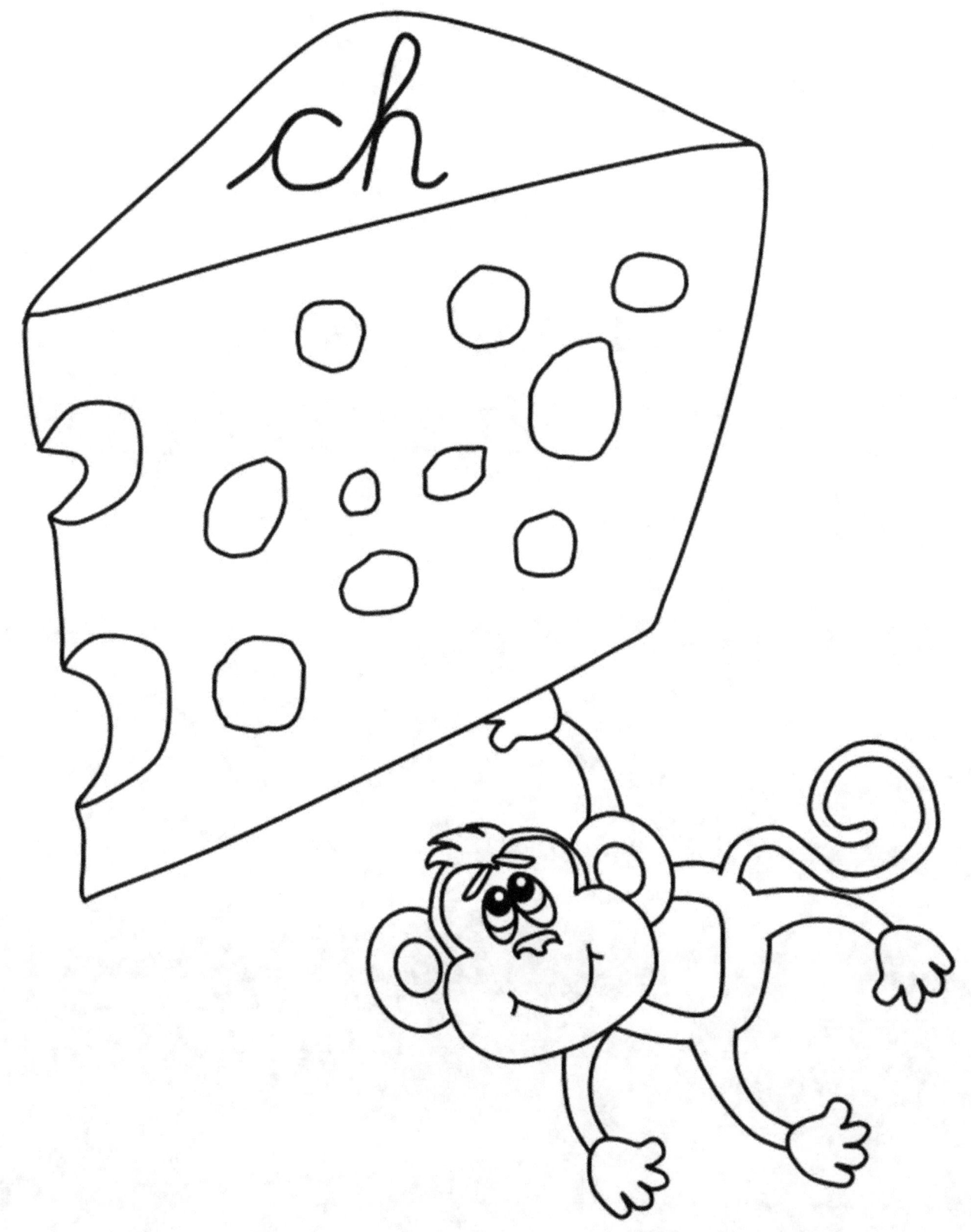

Trace the steps for making the letter c on the following line.

c   h   ch   ch   ch   ch   ch

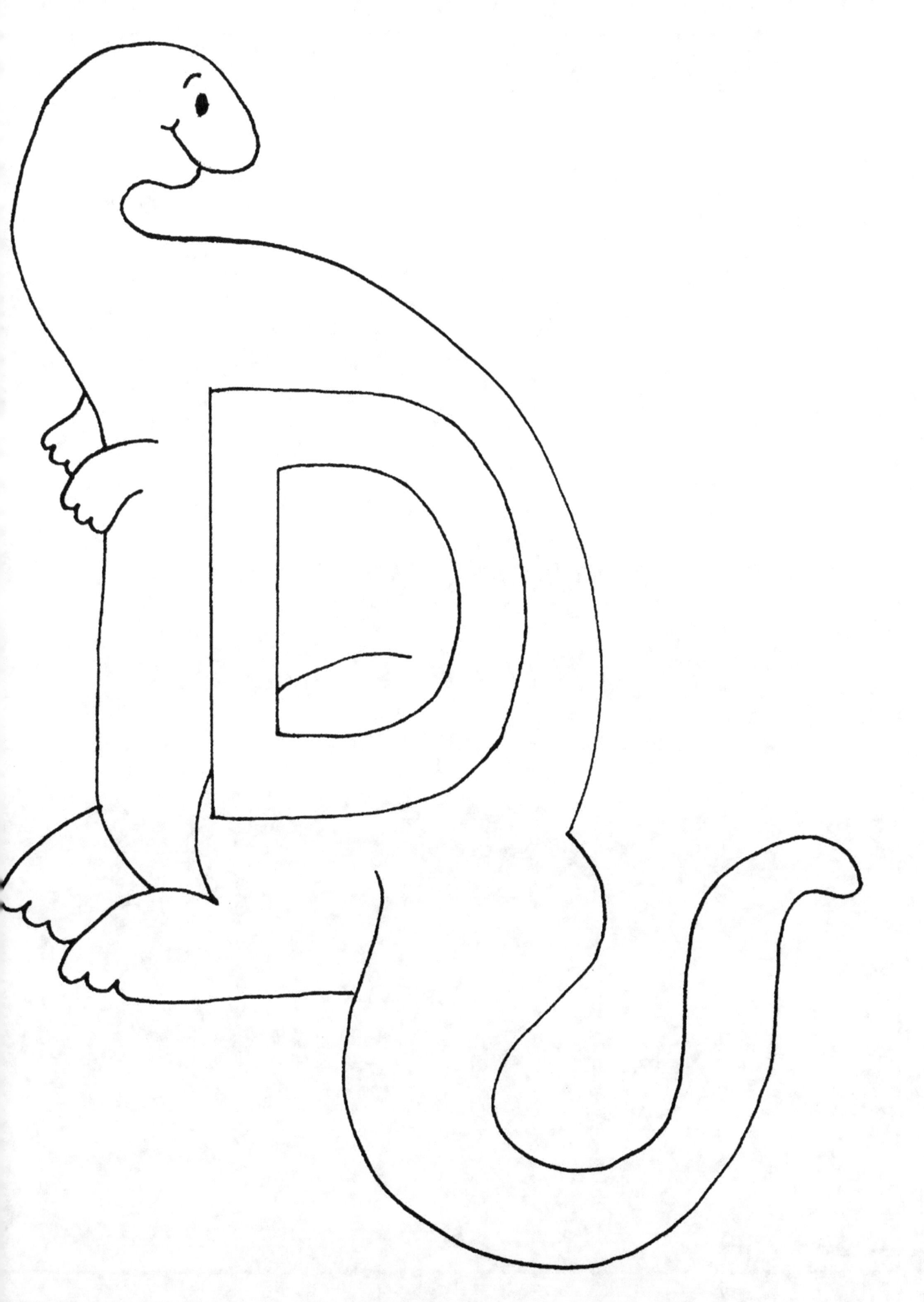

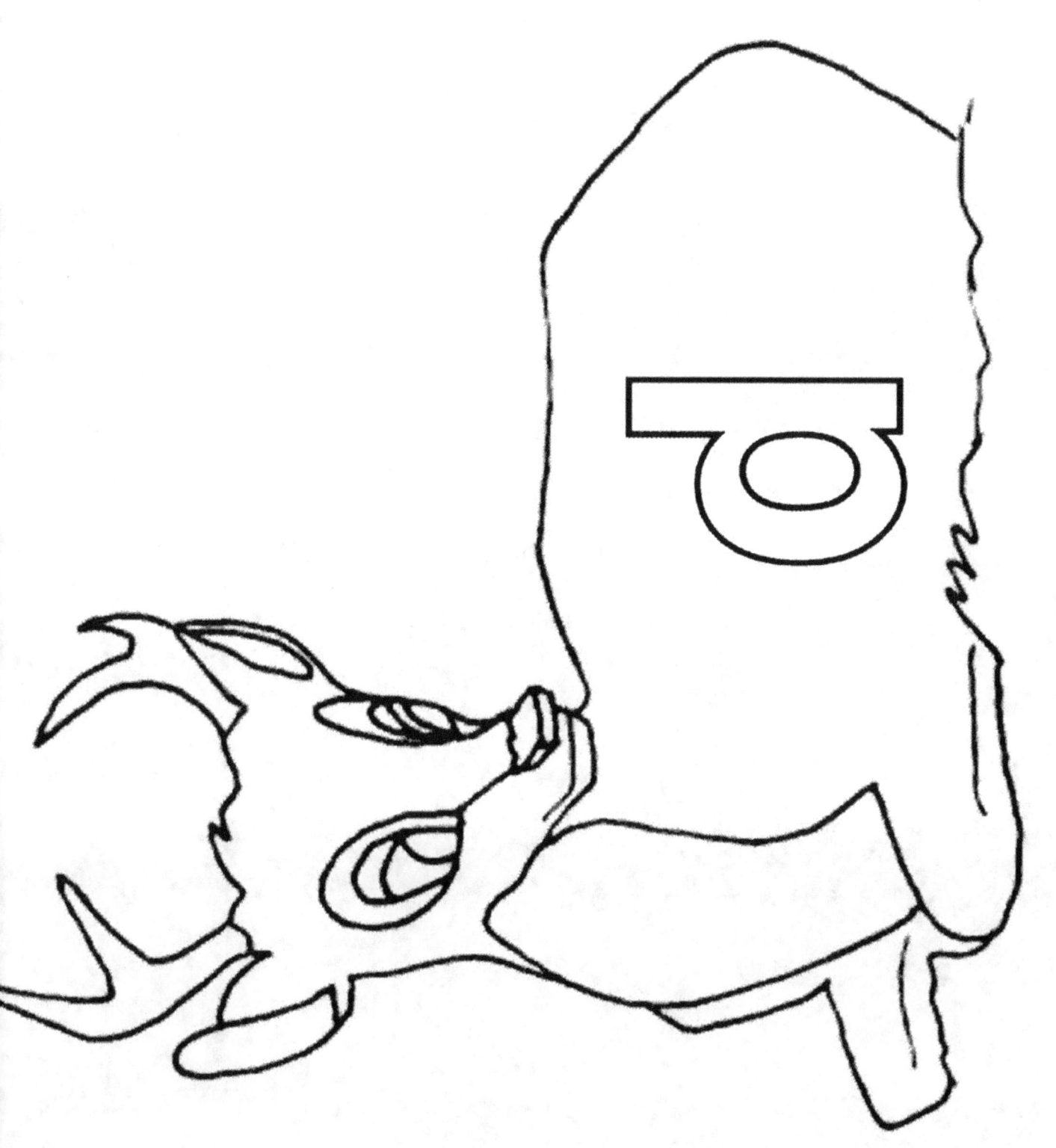

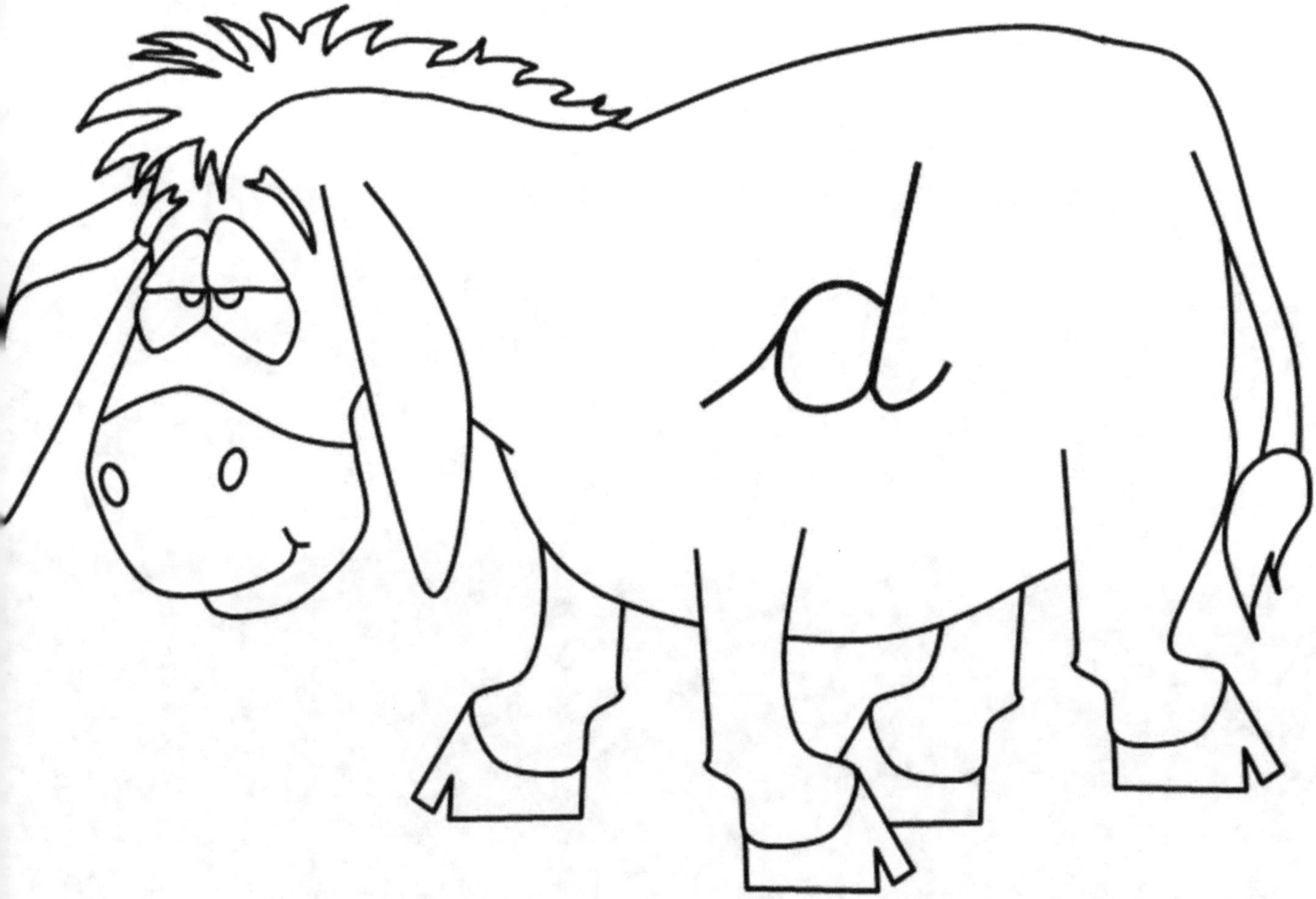

Trace the steps for making the letter d on the following line.

r x d d d d dd

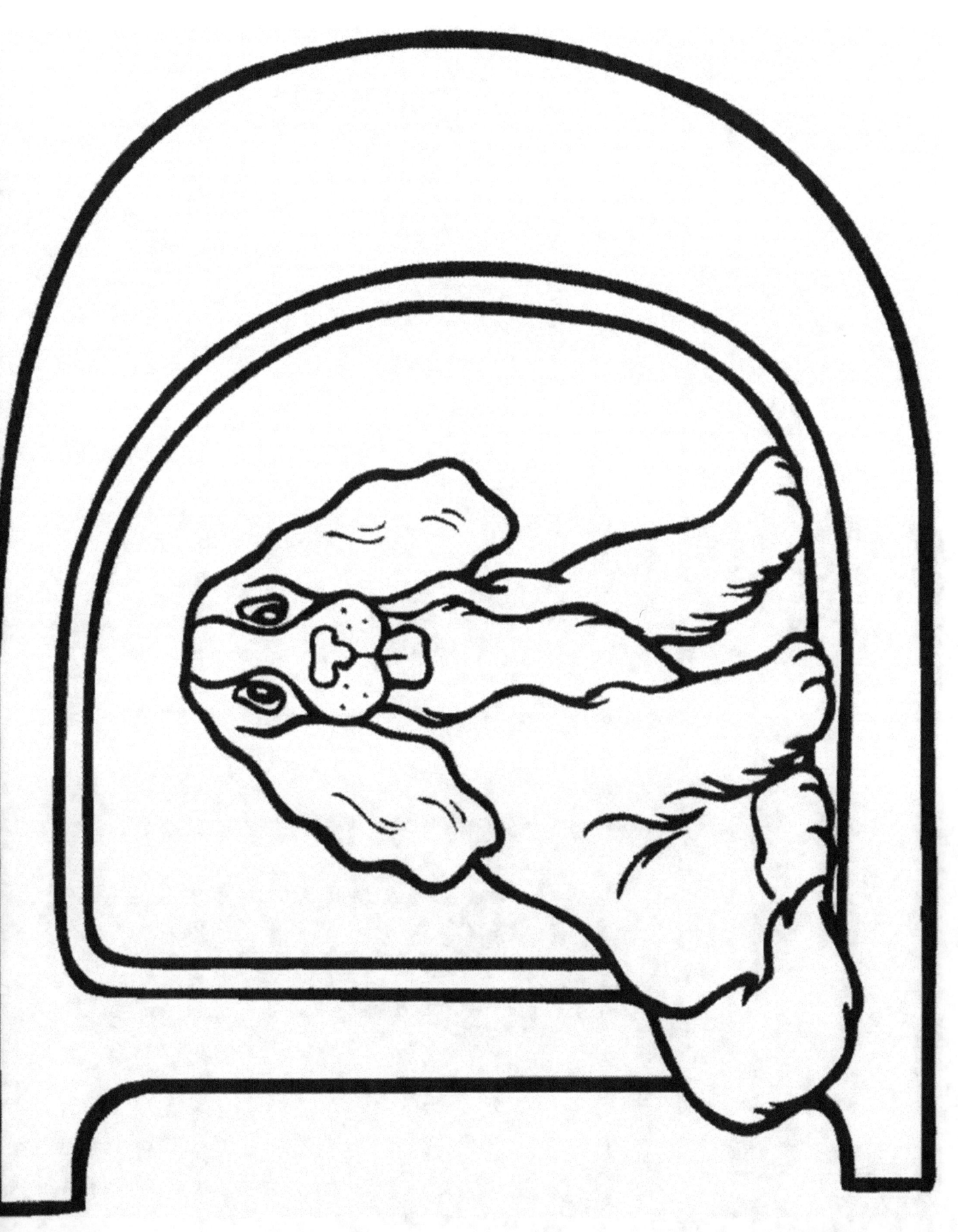

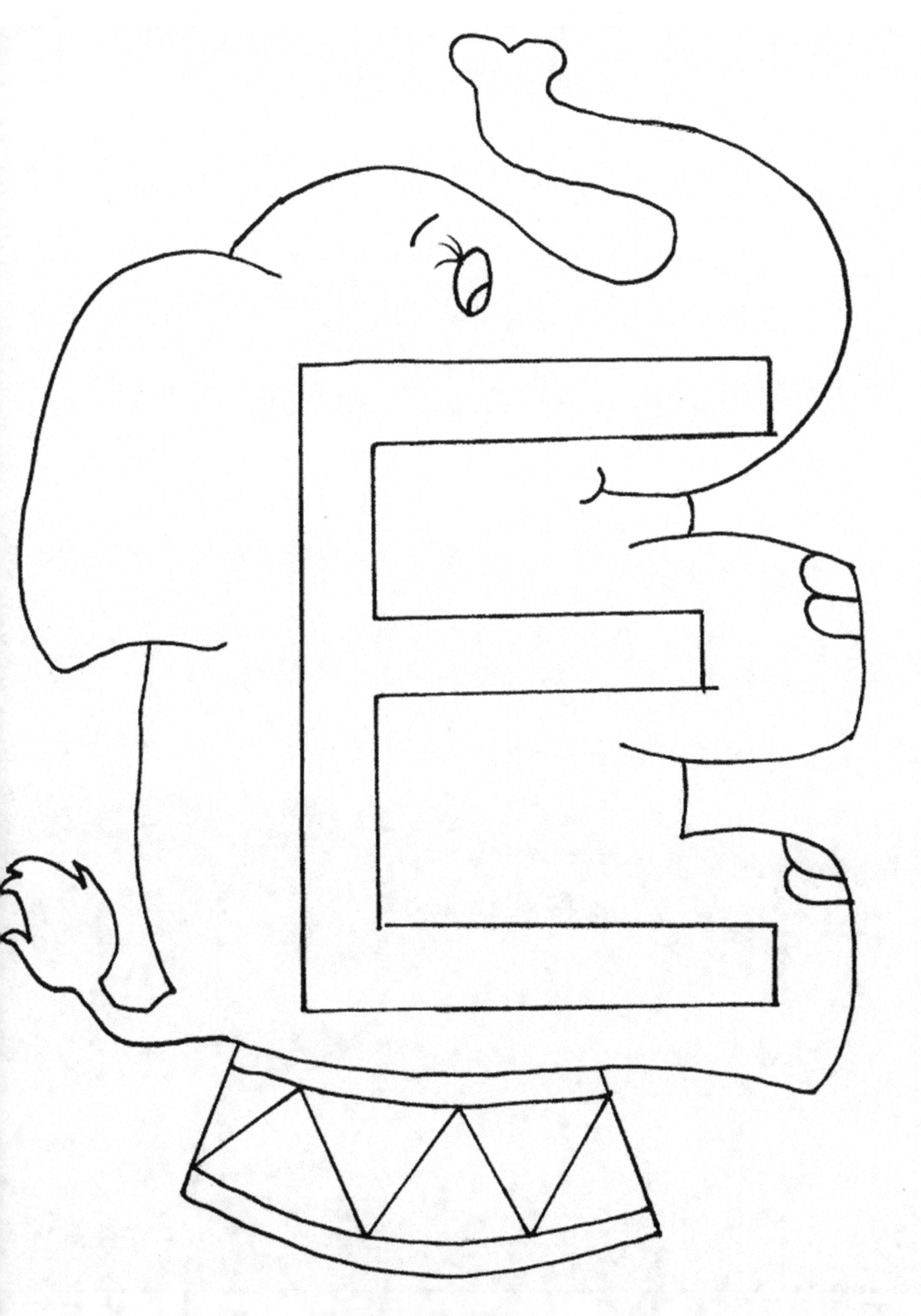

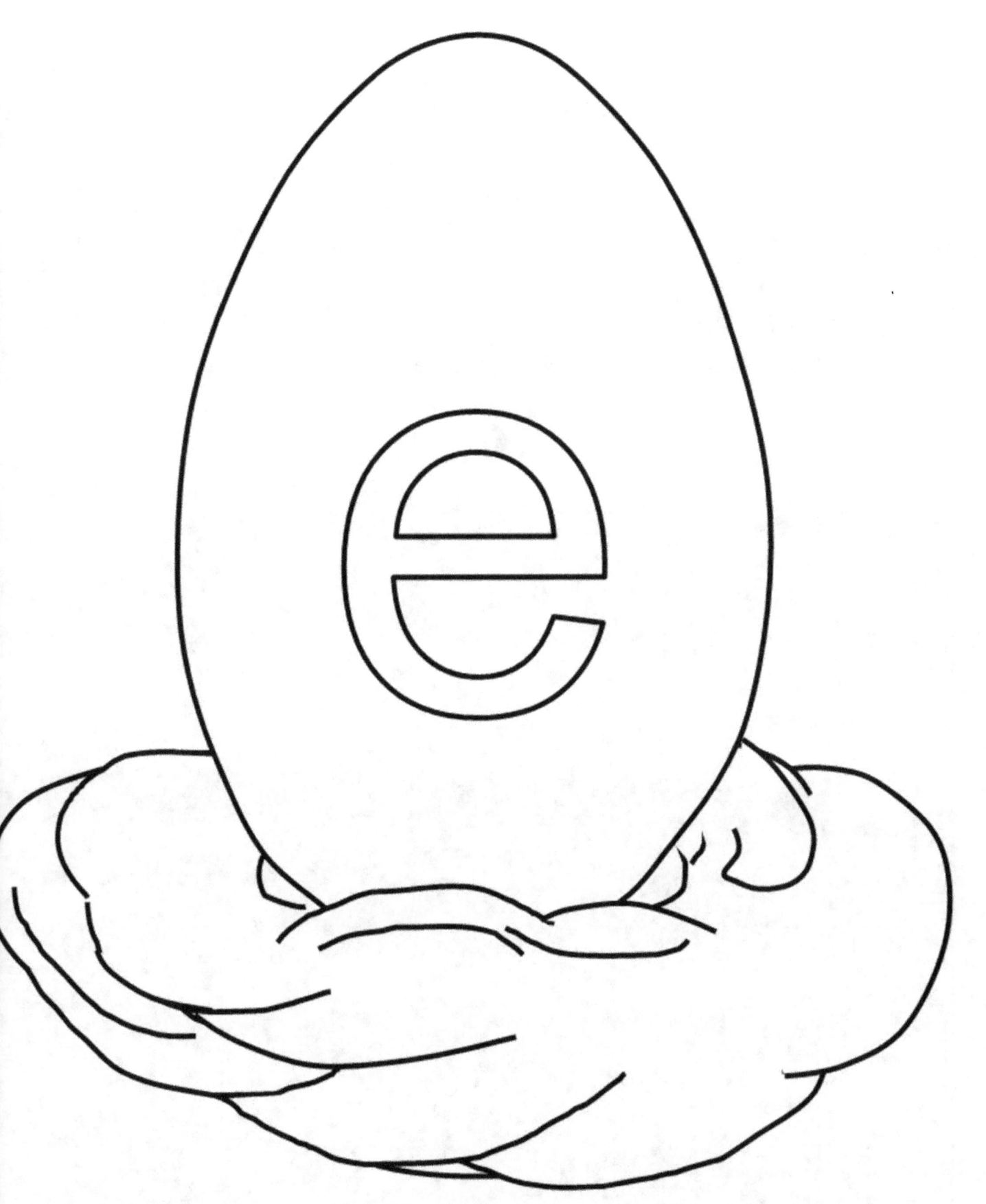

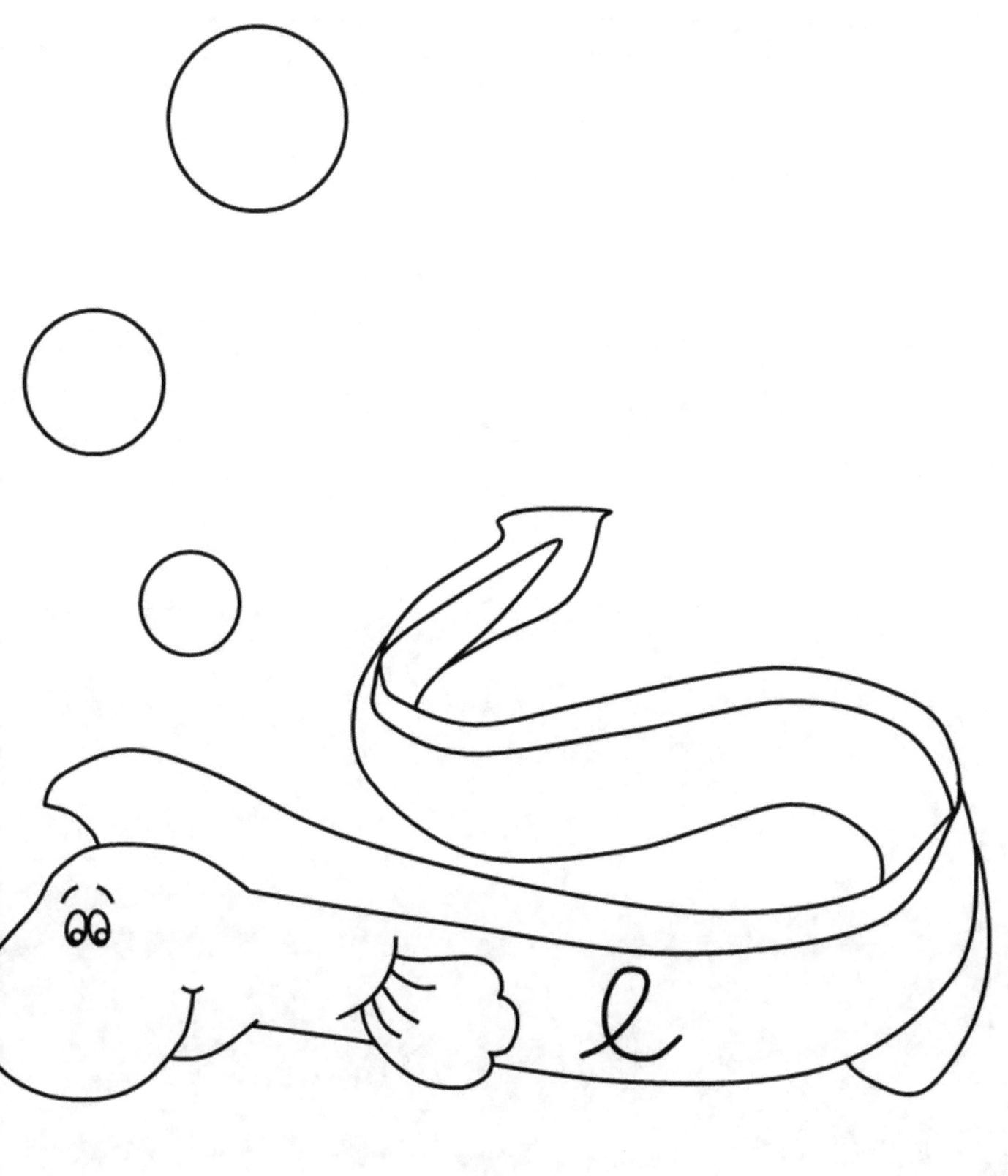

Trace the steps for making the letter e on the following line.

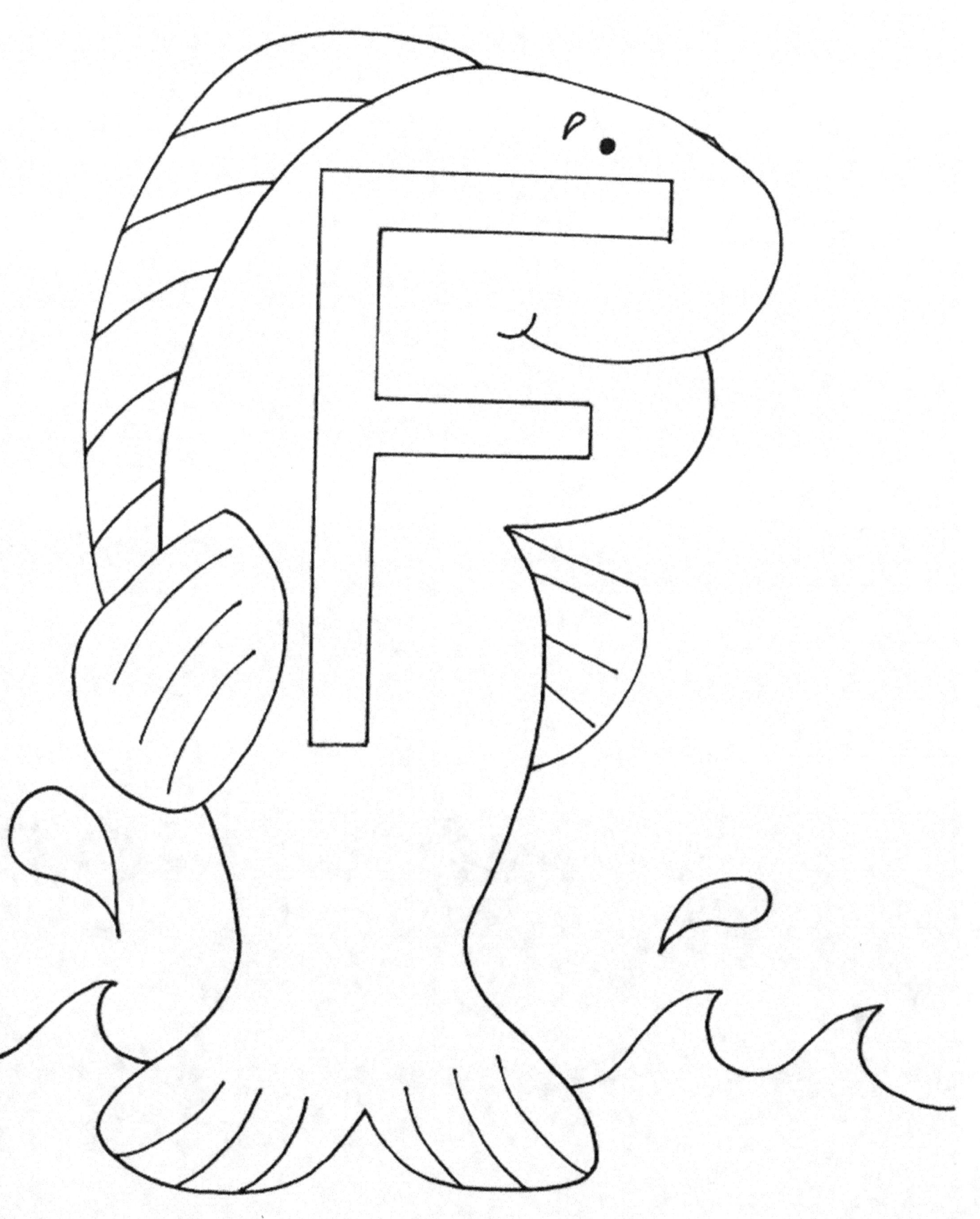

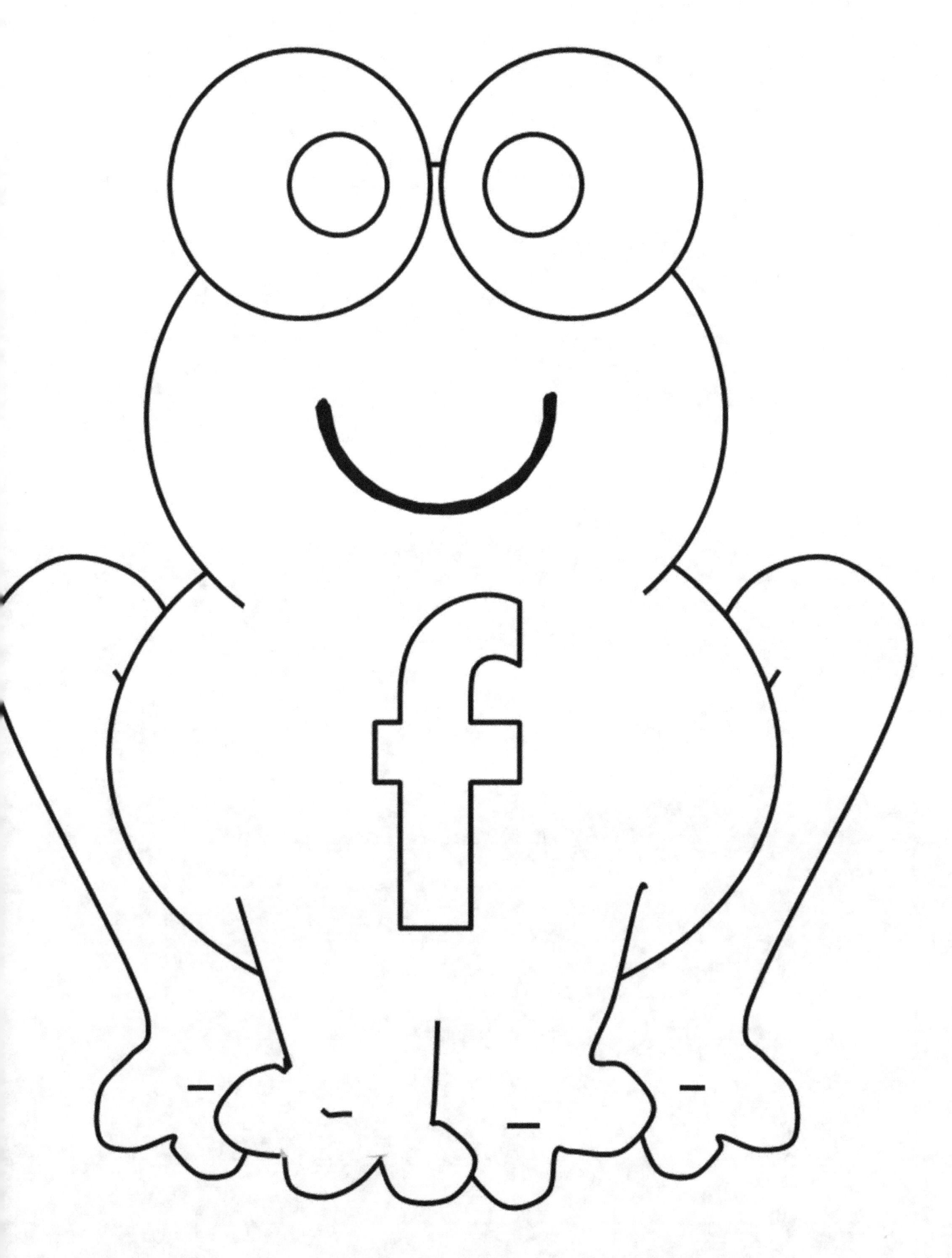

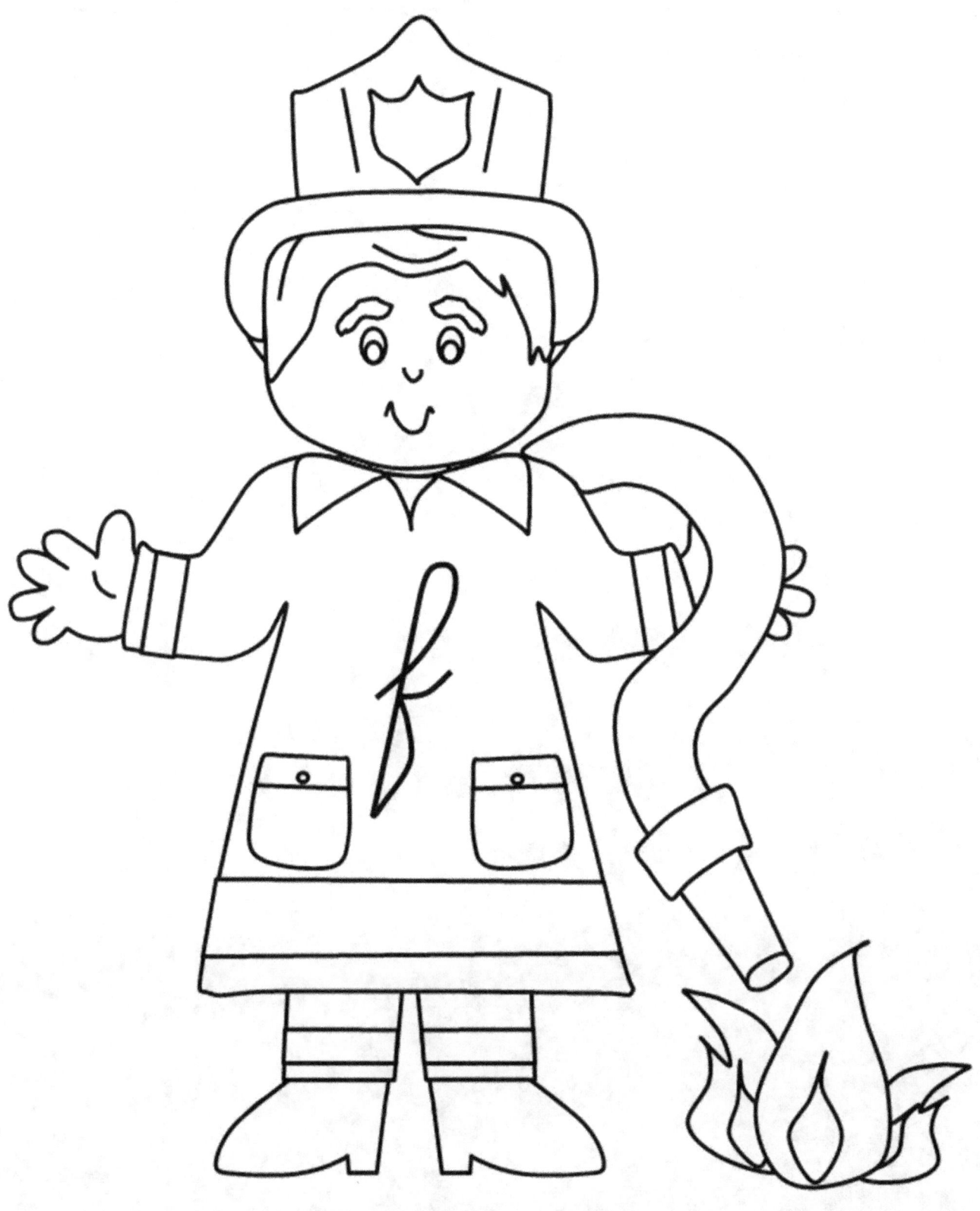

Trace the steps for making the letter f on the following line.

f — f — f — f — f — f — ff

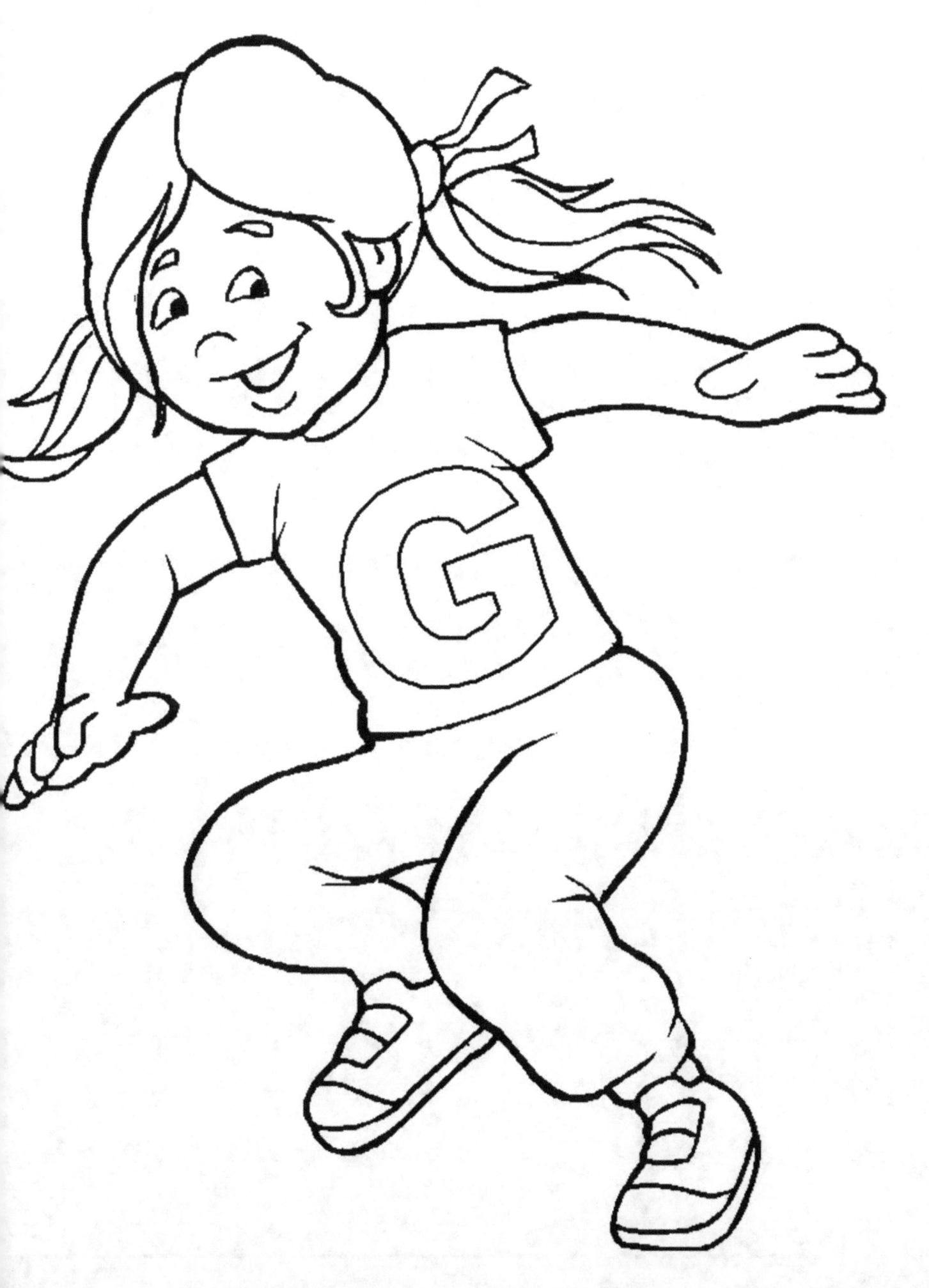

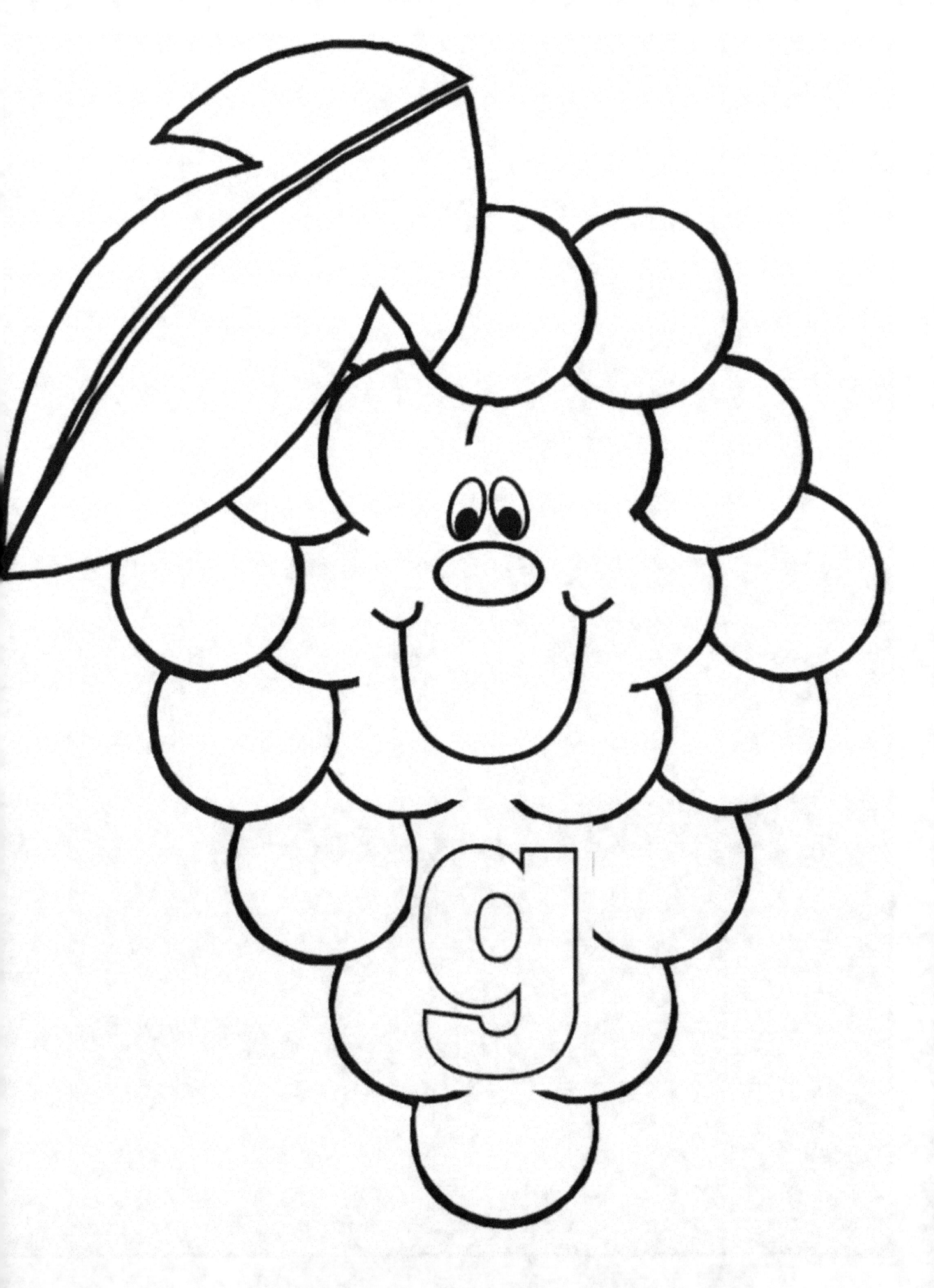

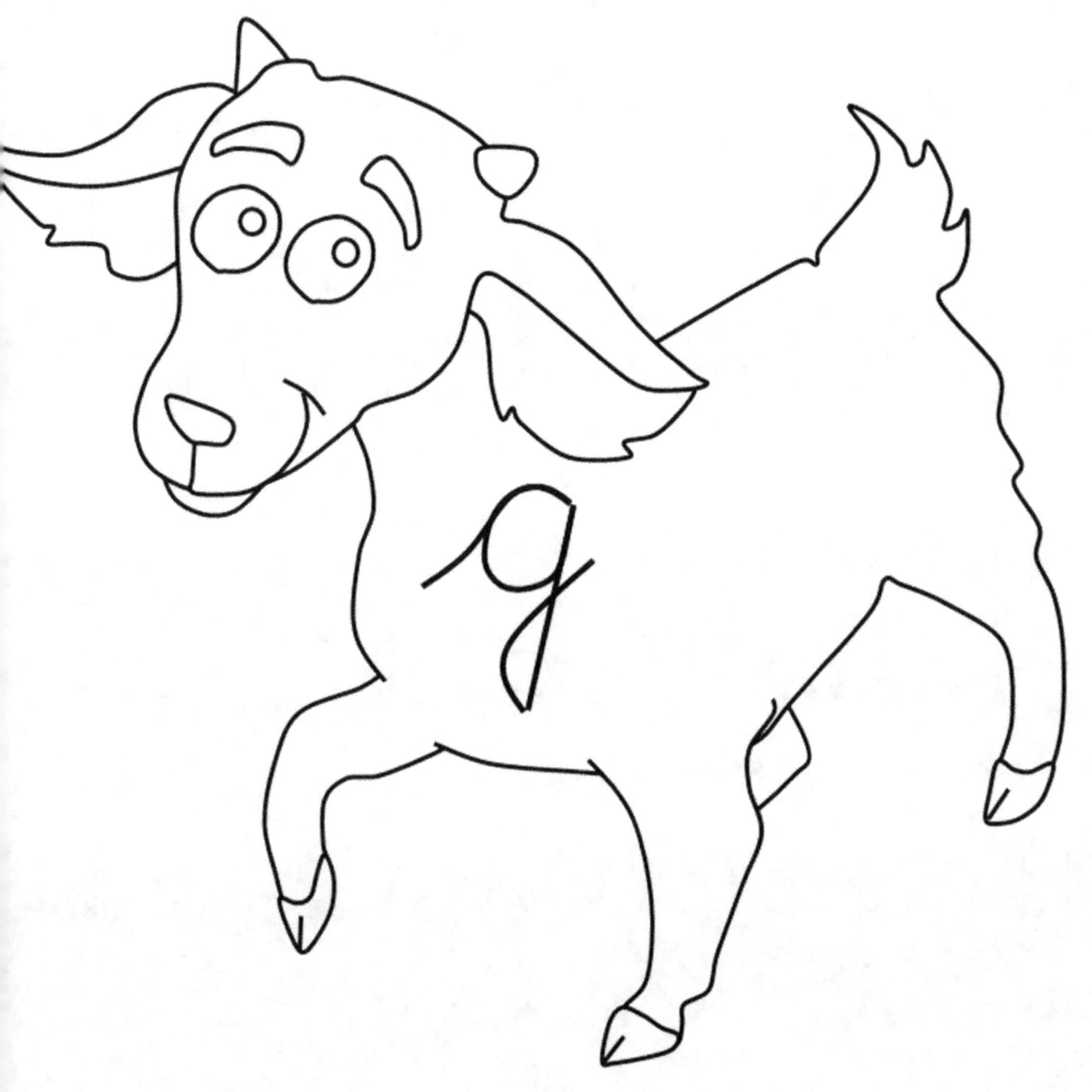

Trace the steps for making the letter g on the following line.

$\mathcal{G} \quad \mathcal{G} \quad \mathcal{G} \quad \mathcal{G} \quad \mathcal{G} \quad \mathcal{G} \quad \mathcal{G} \quad \mathcal{G}$

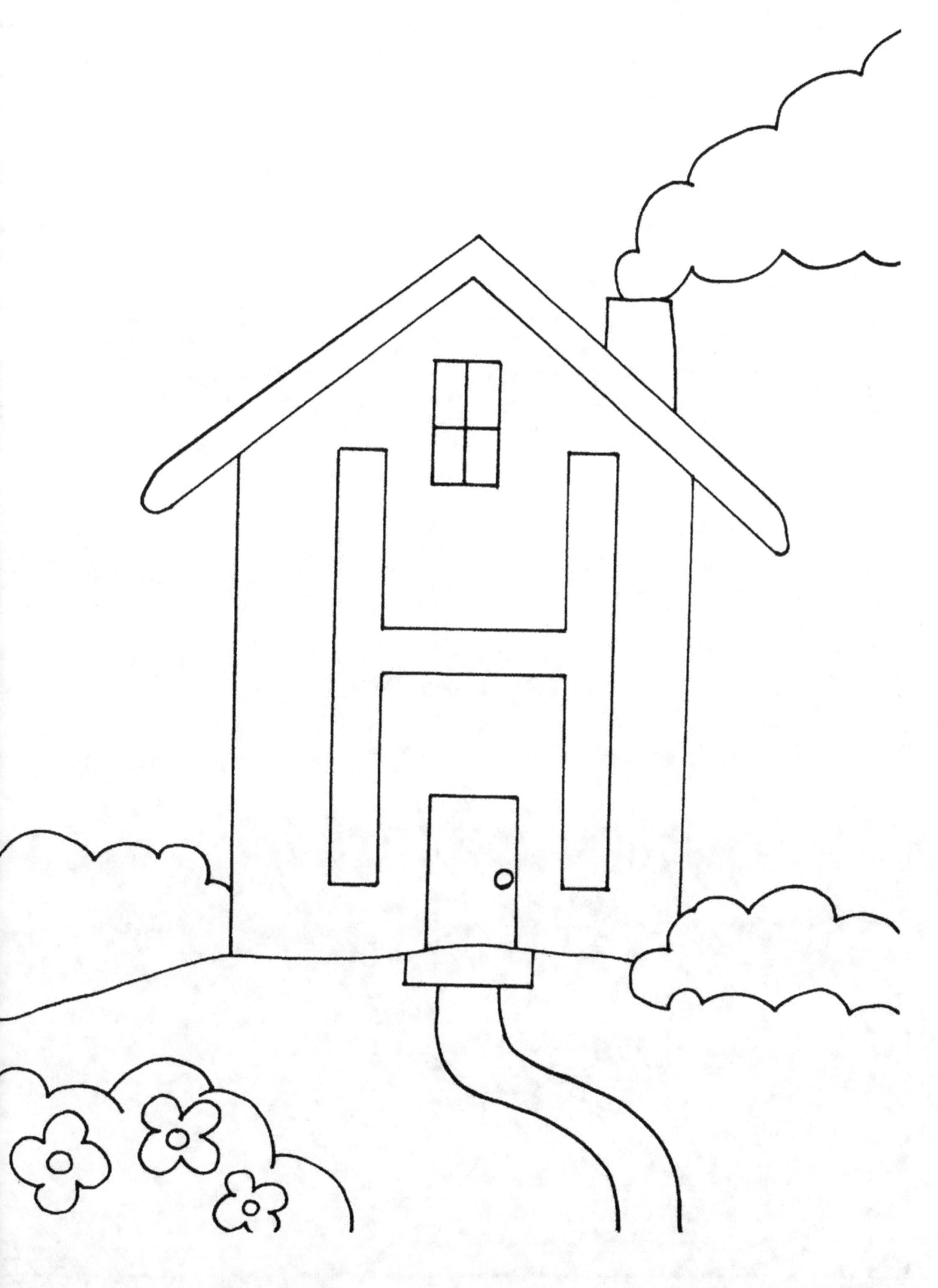

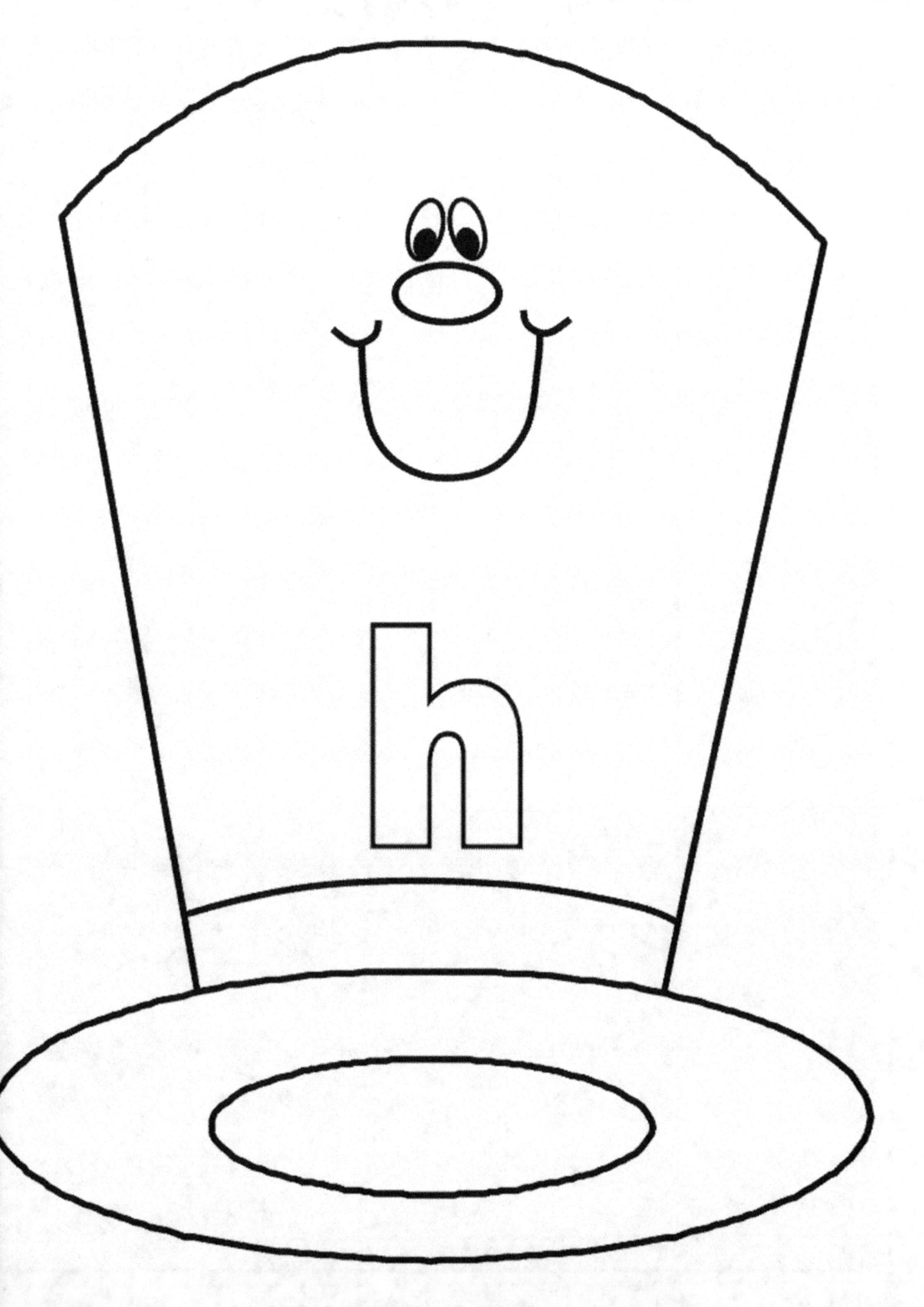

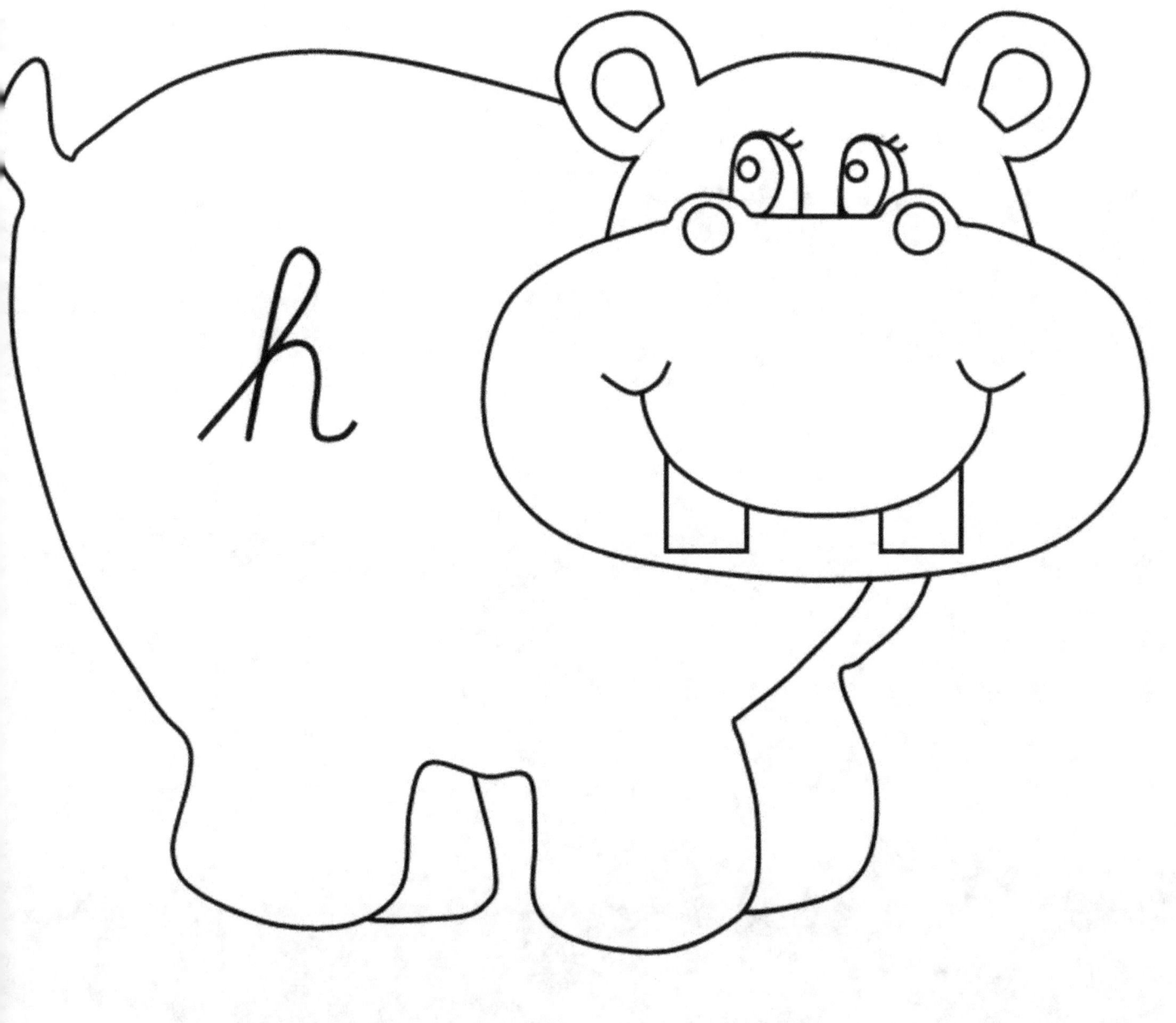

Trace the steps for making the letter h on the following line.

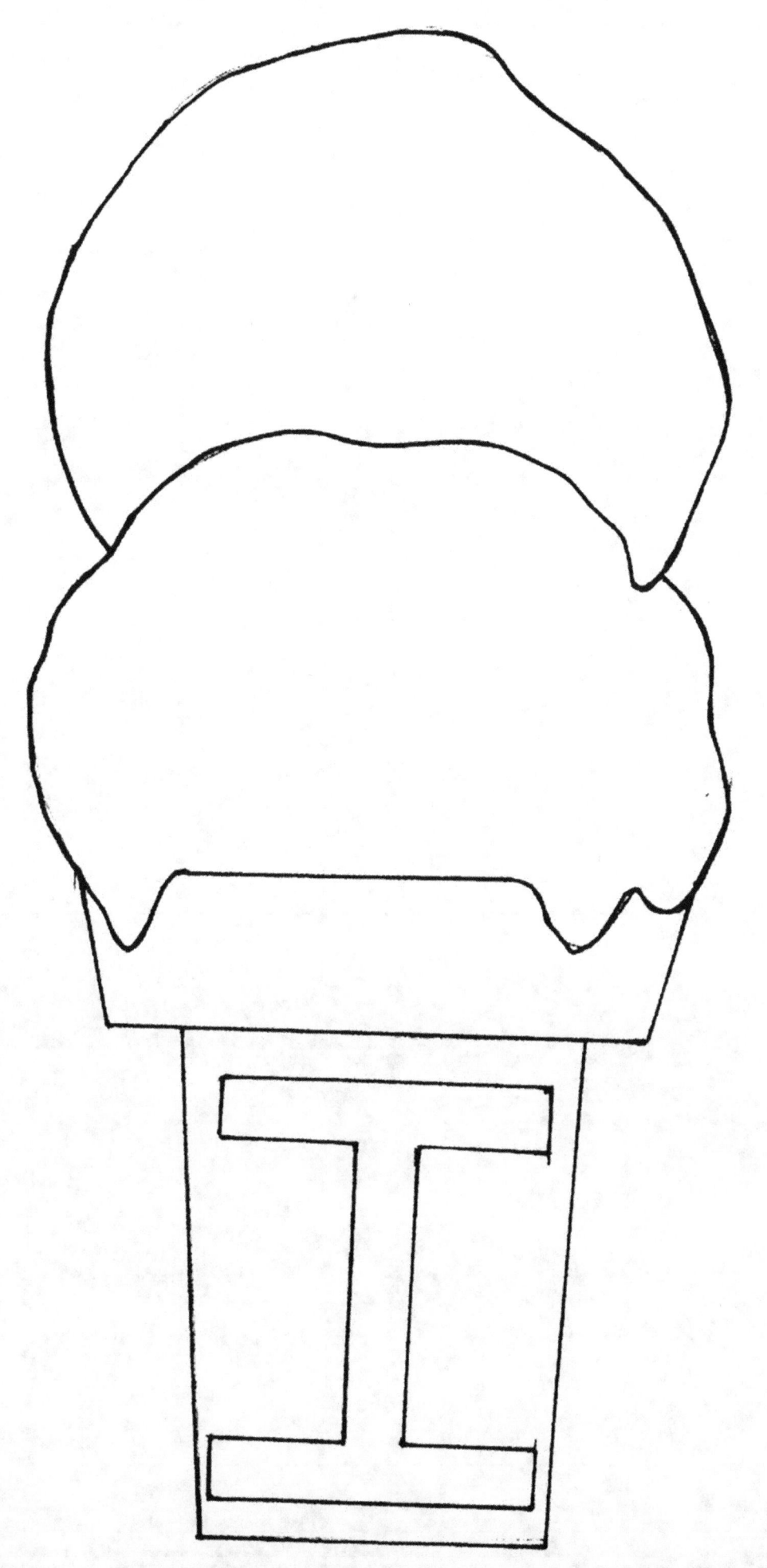

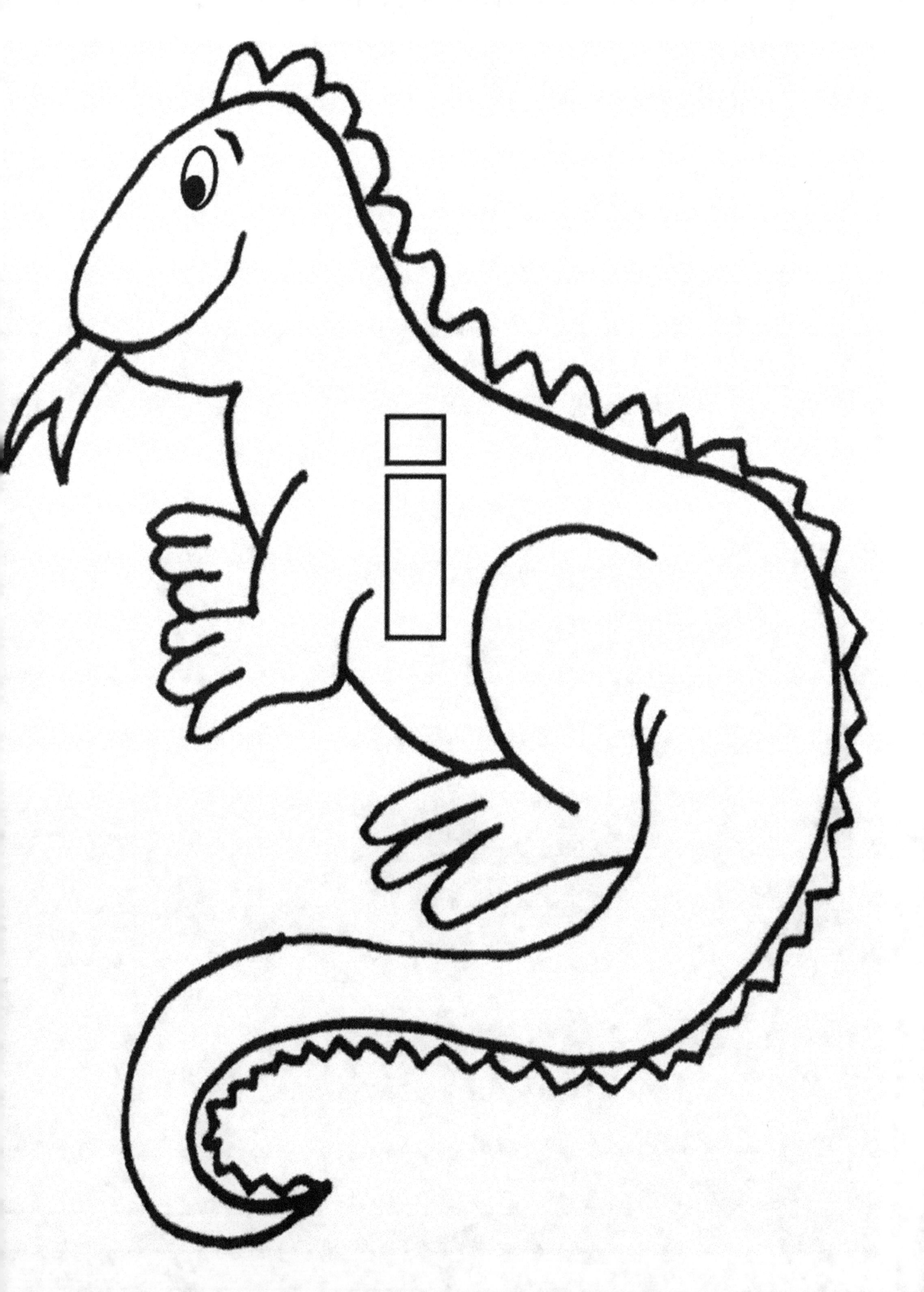

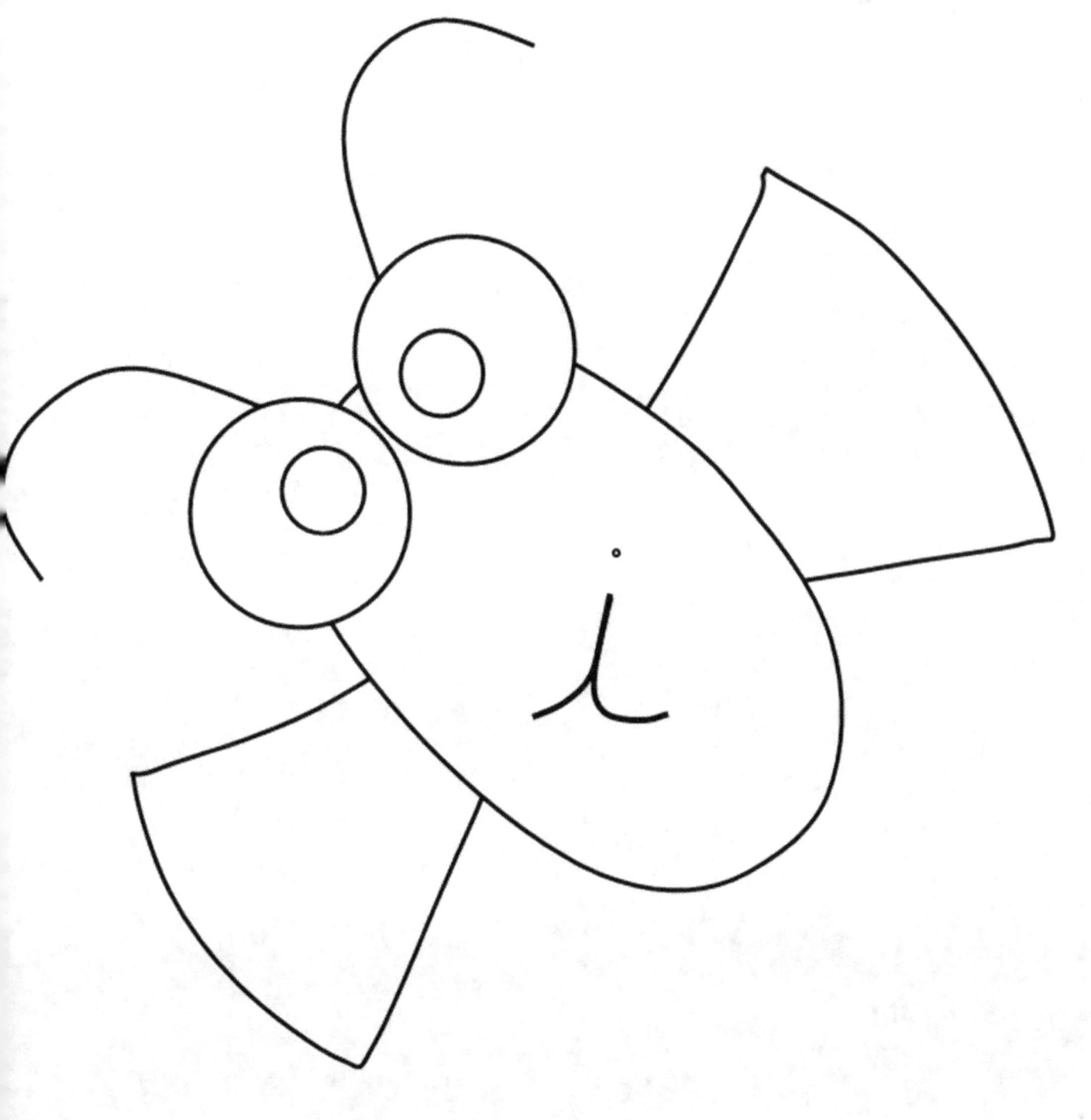

race the steps for making the letter i on the following line.

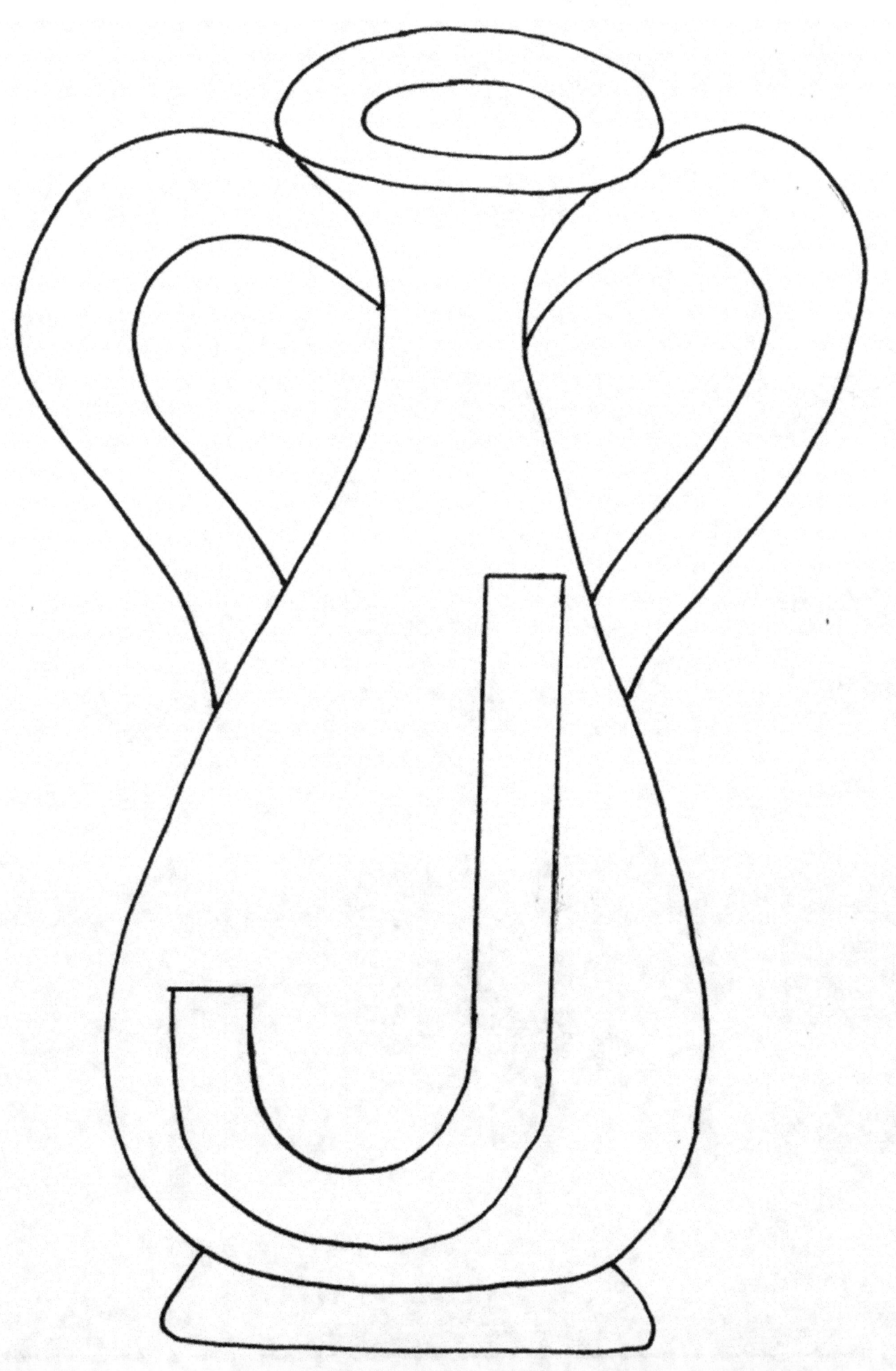

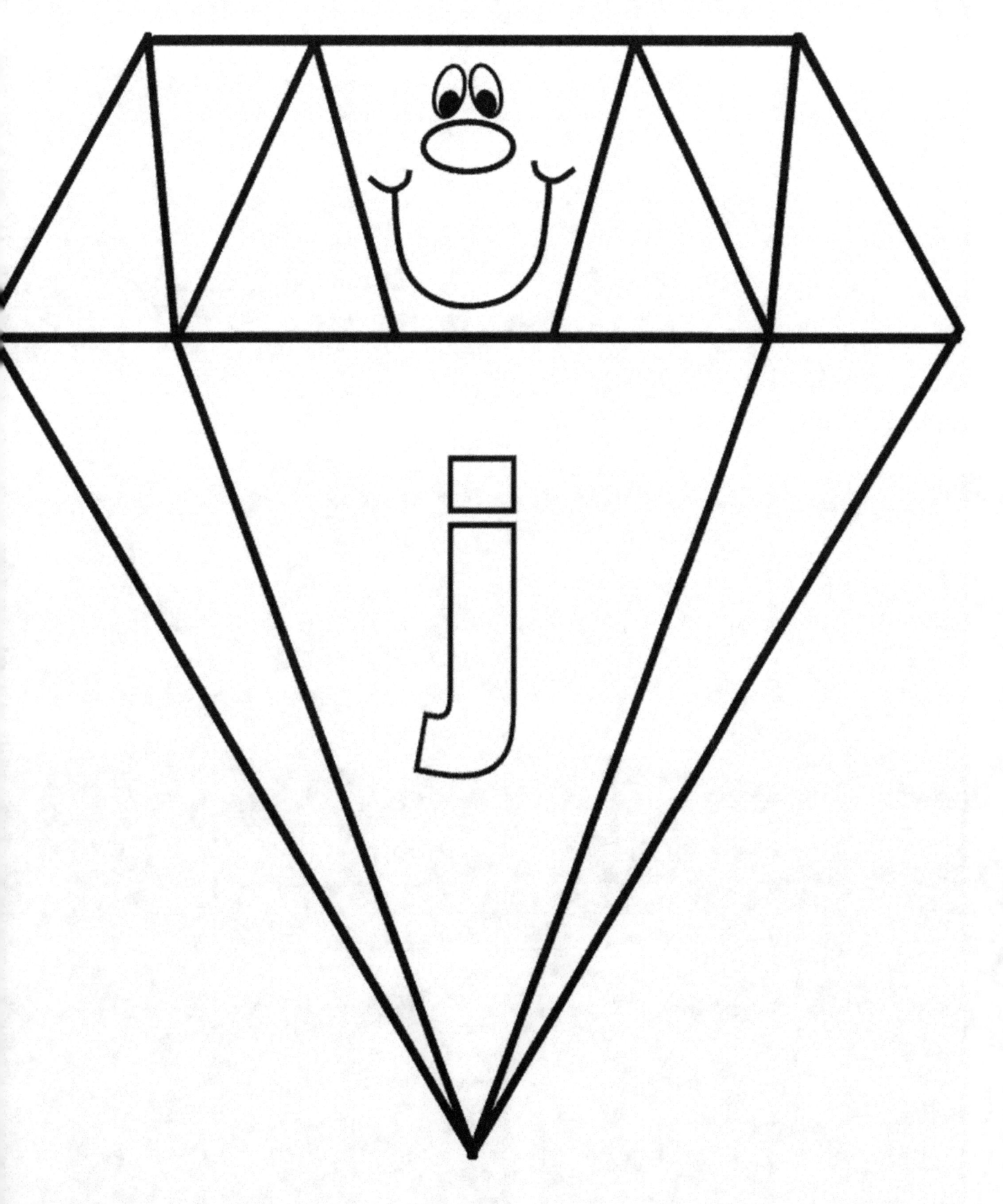

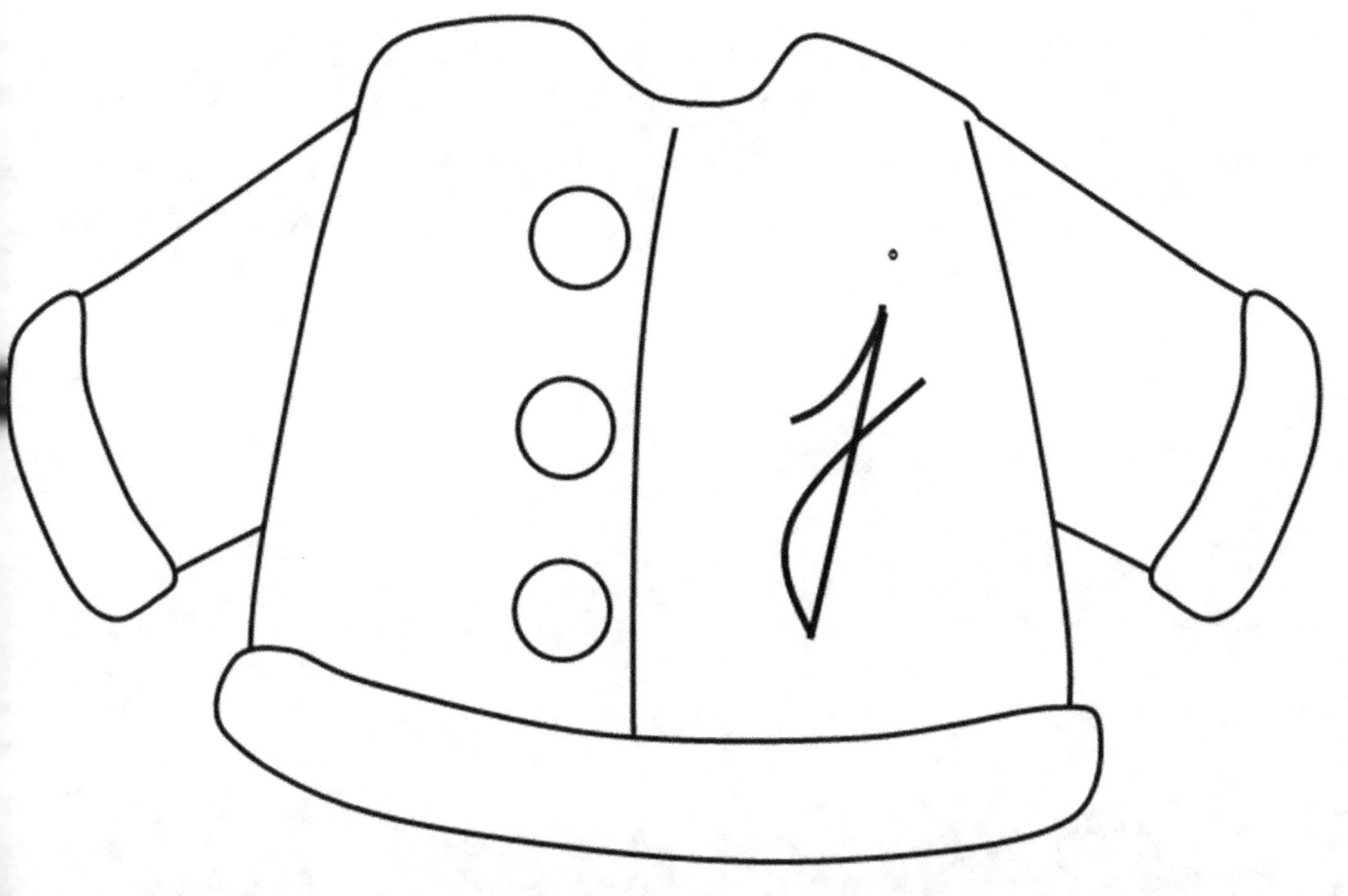

Trace the steps for making the letter j on the following line.

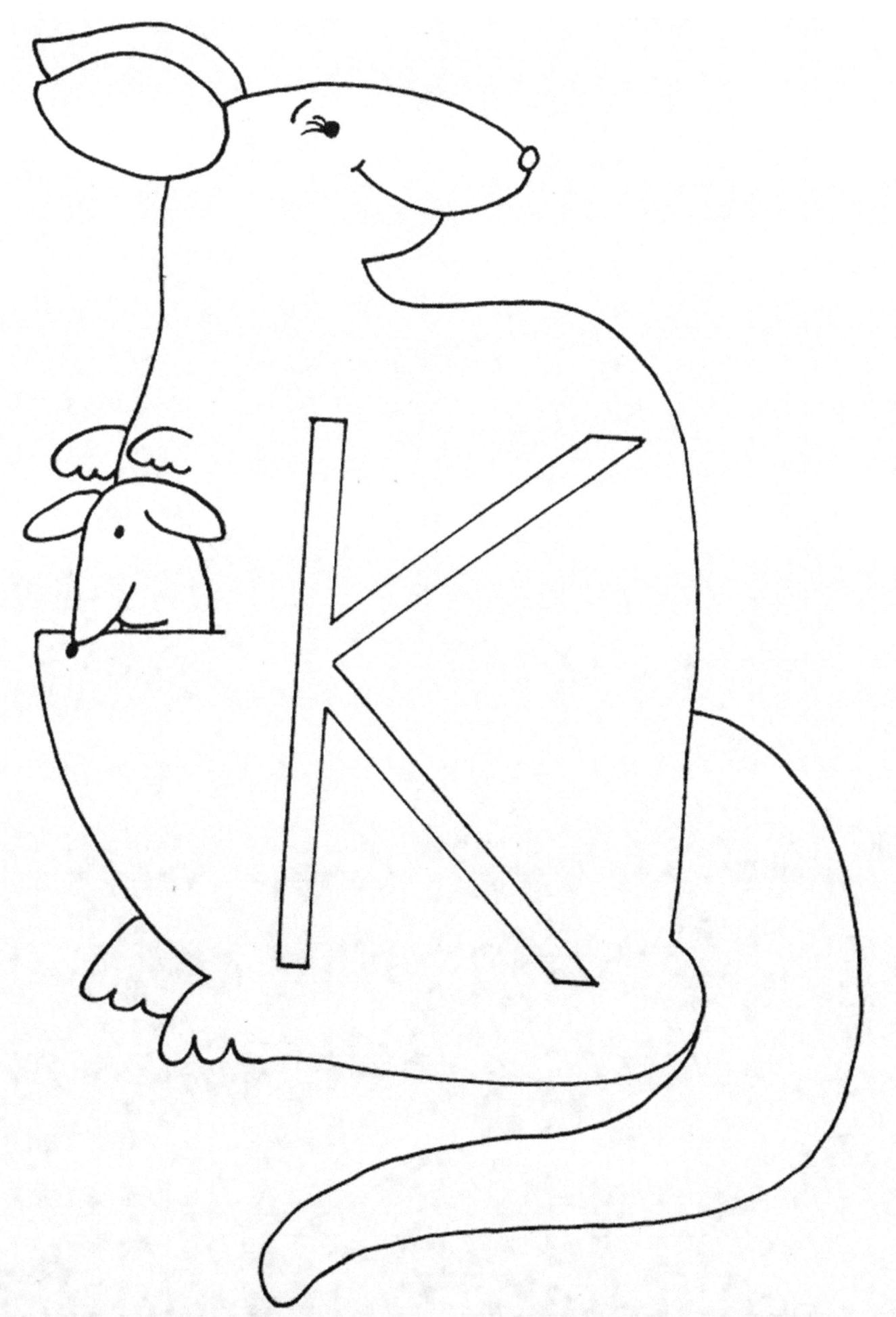

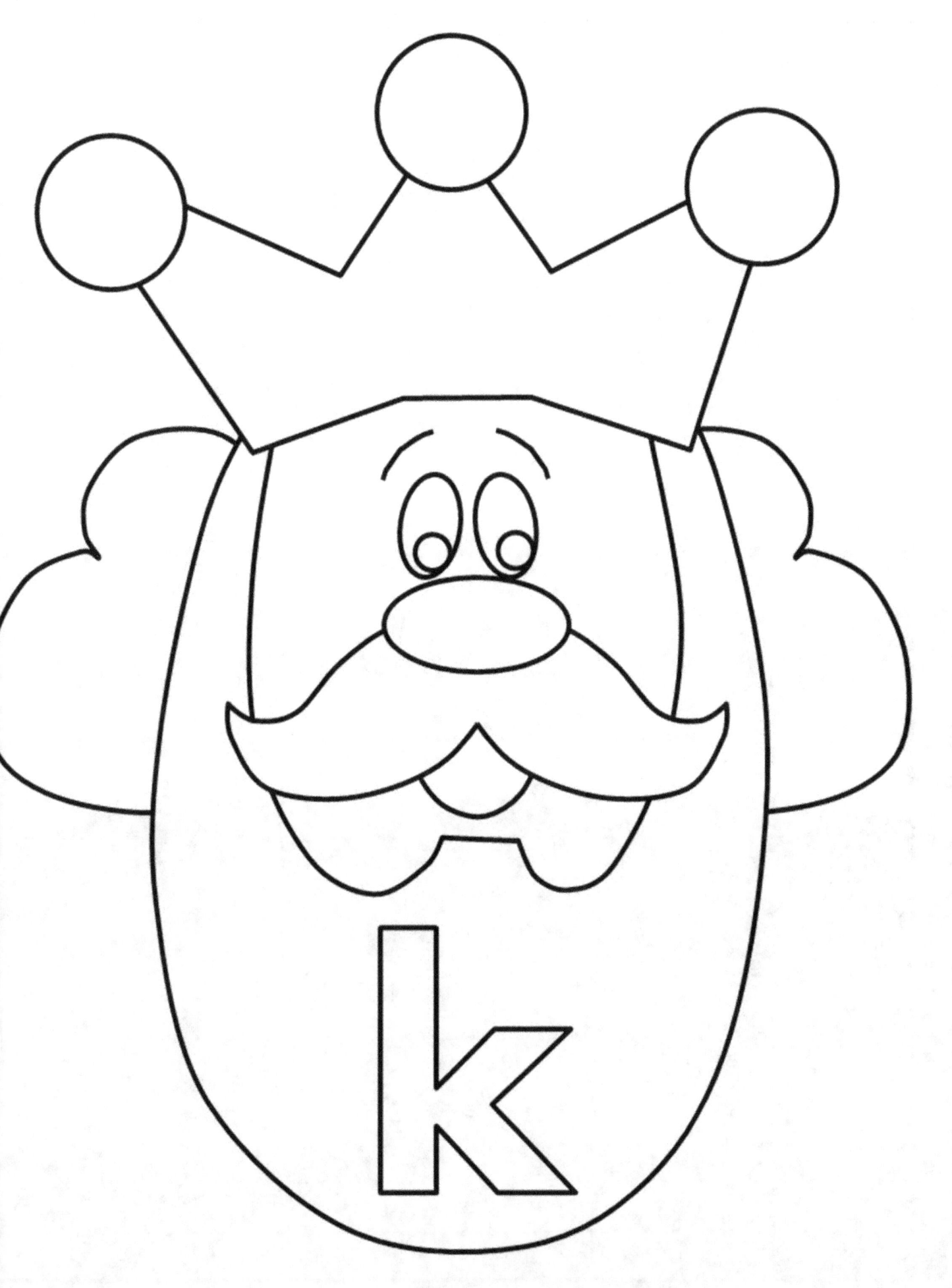

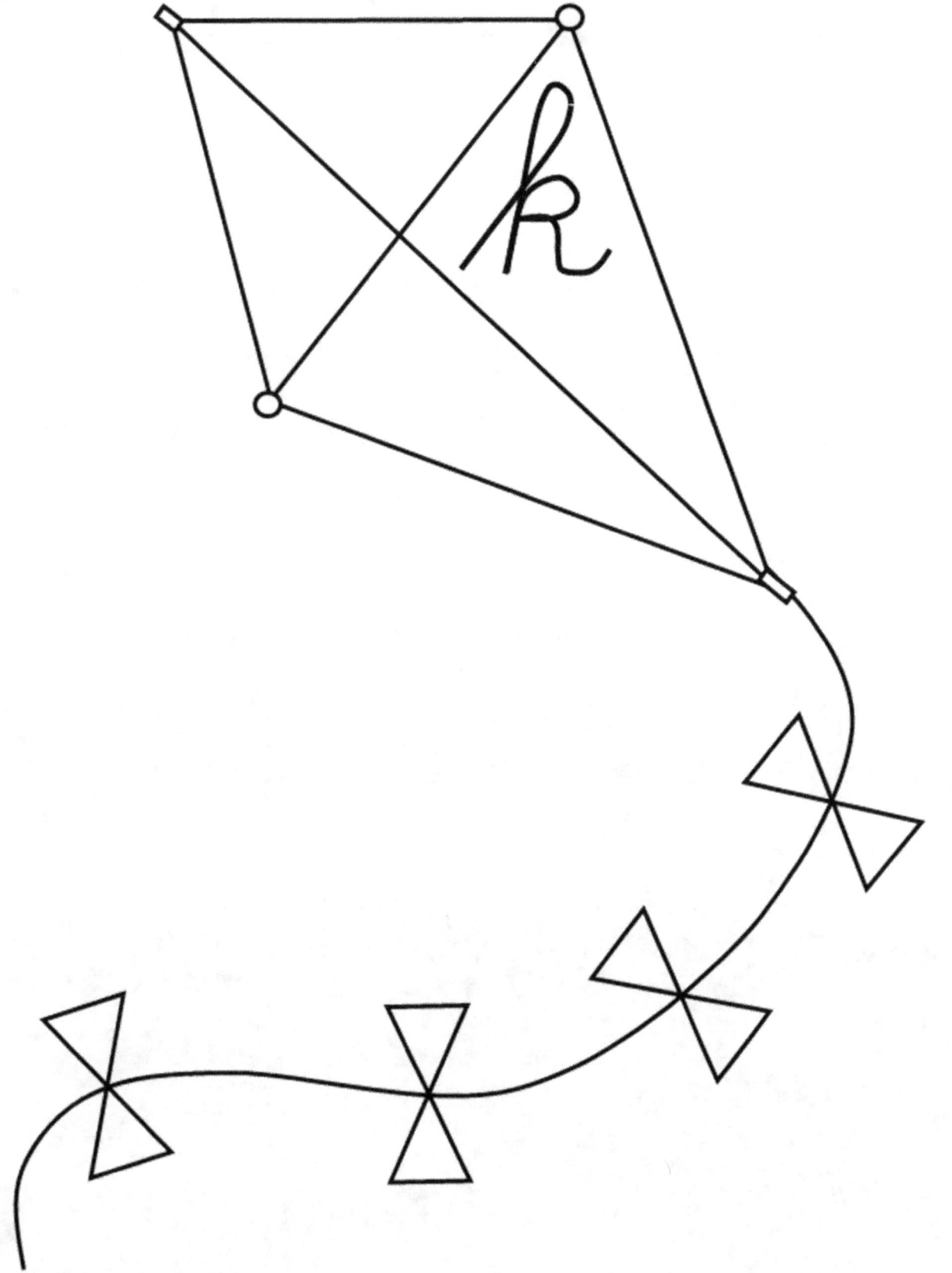

Trace the steps for making the letter k on the following line.

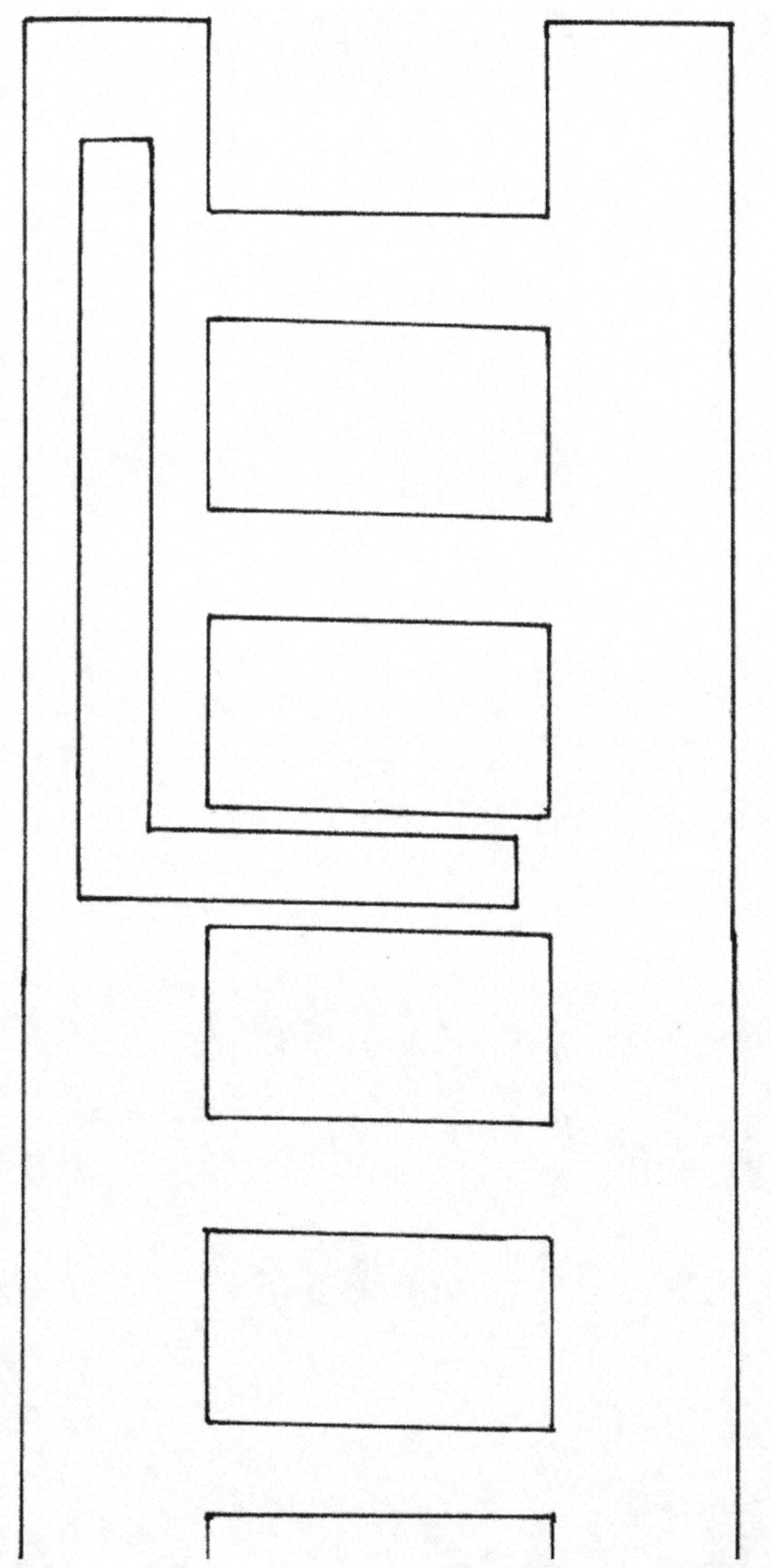

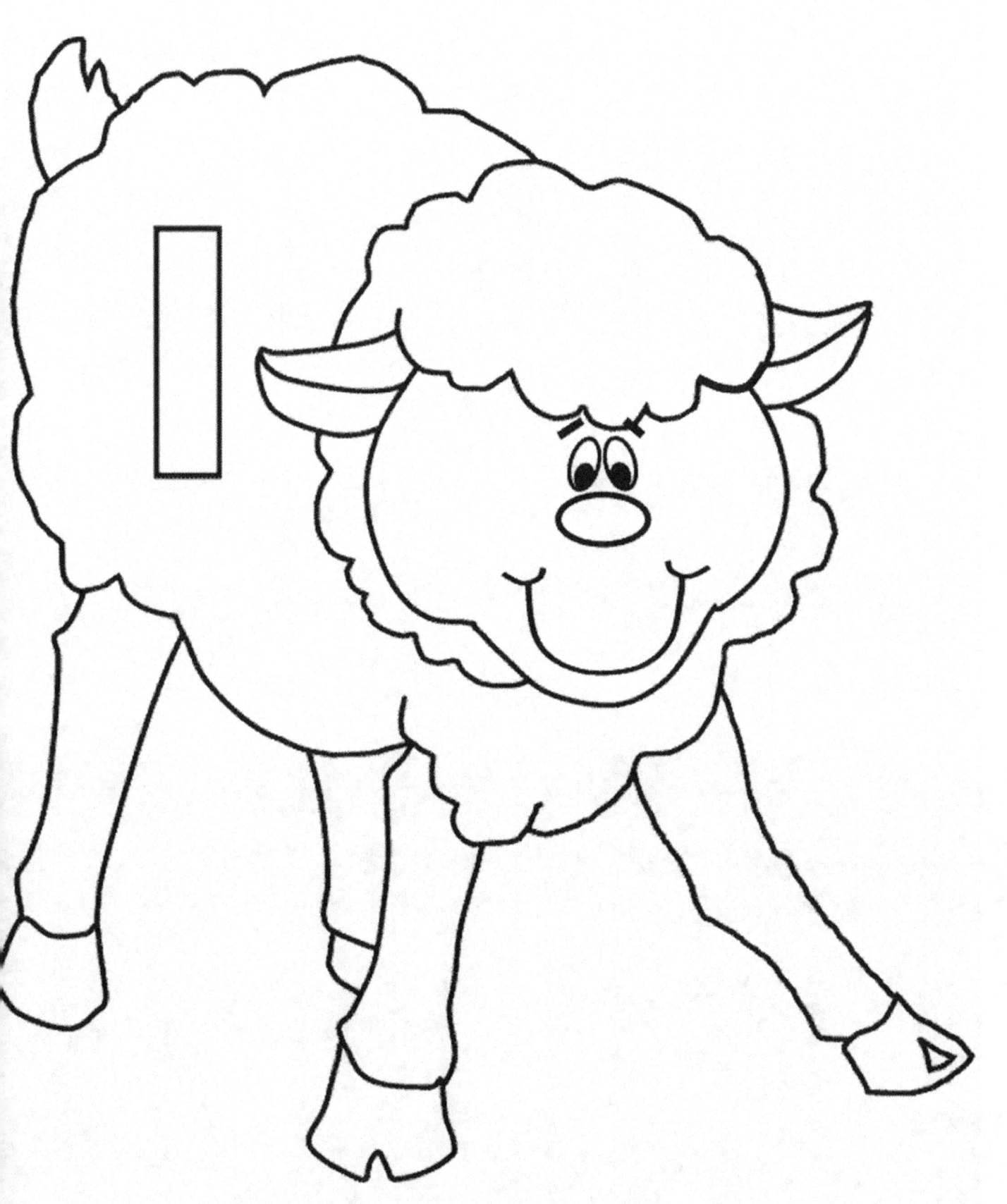

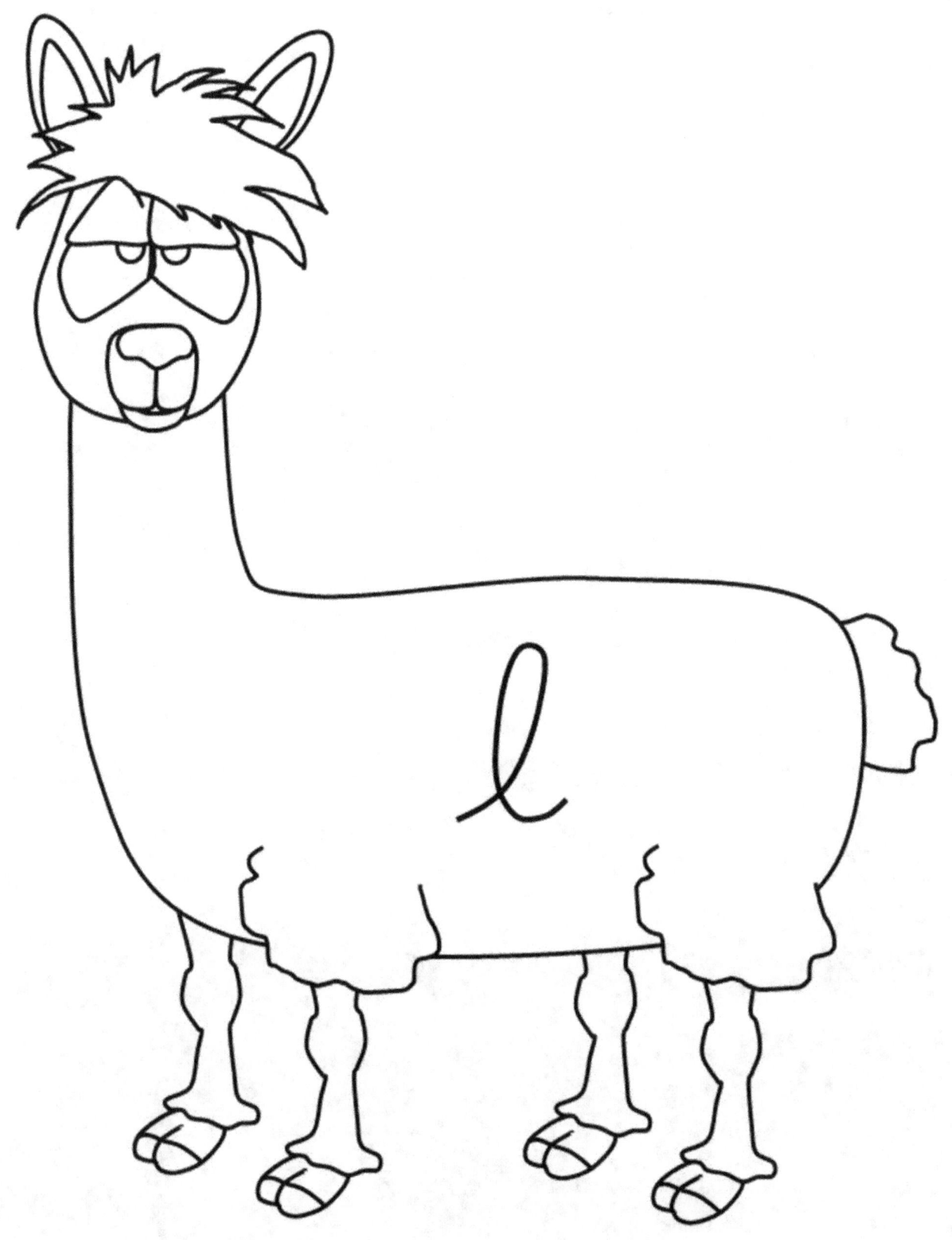

Trace the steps for making the letter l on the following line.

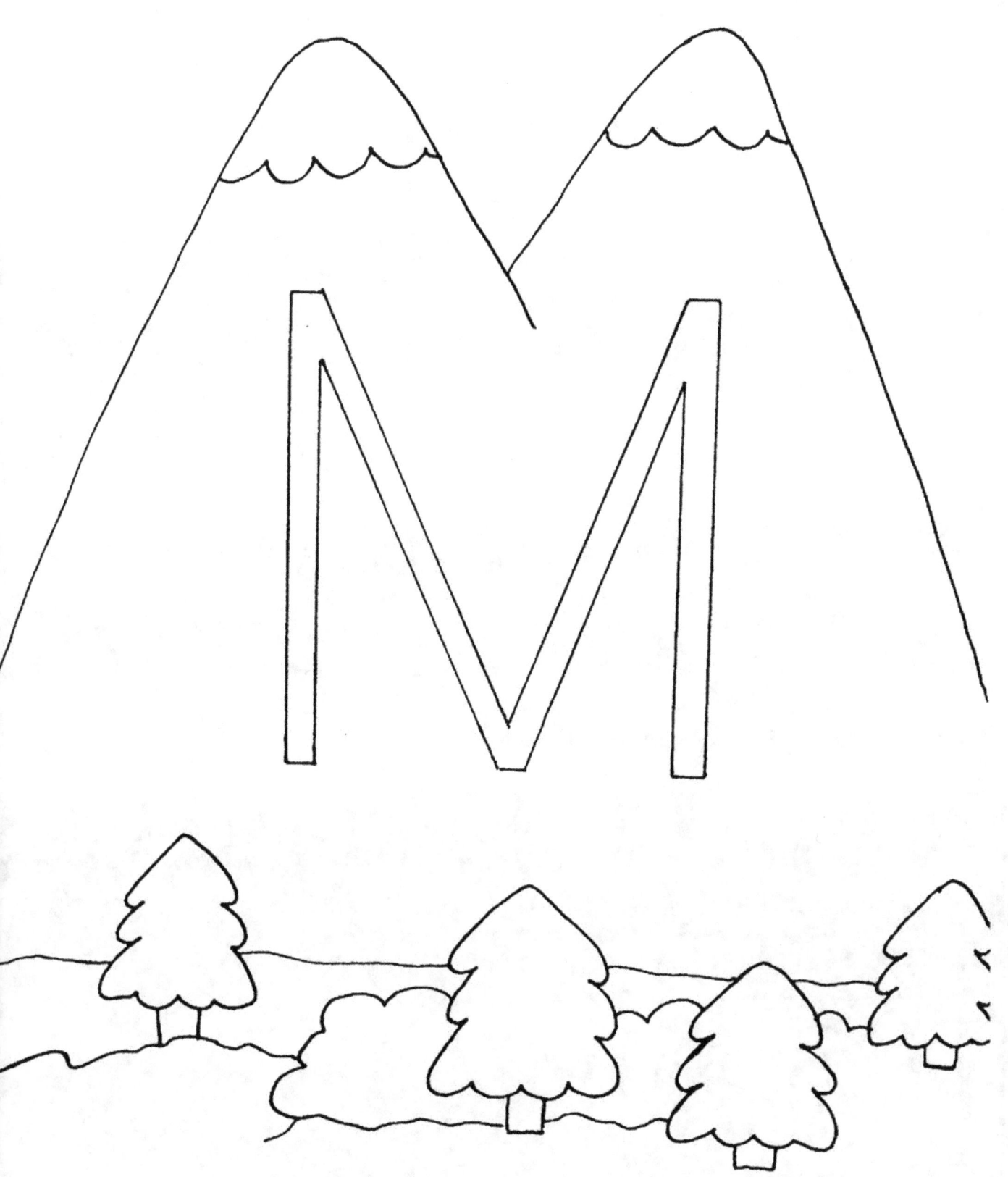

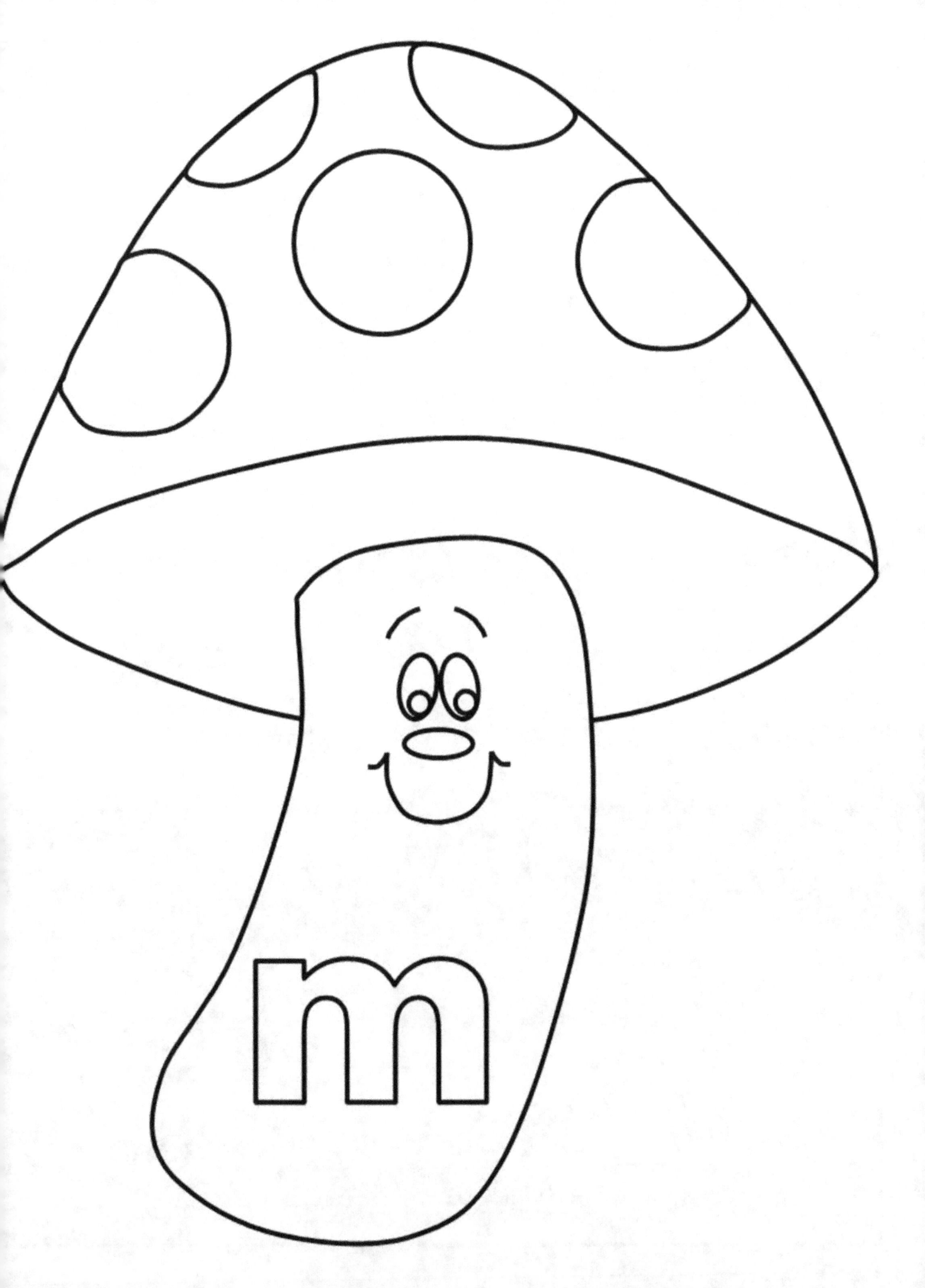

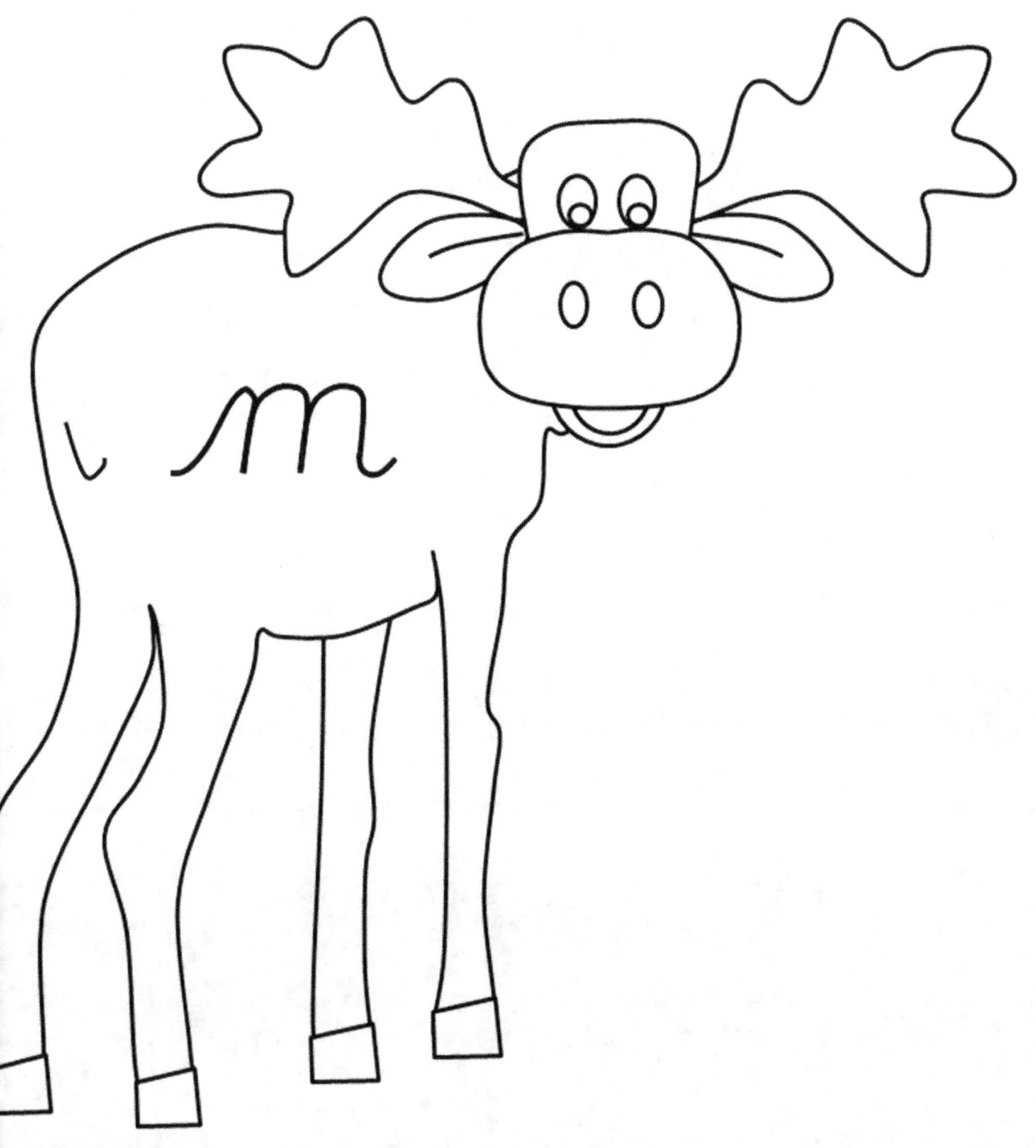

Trace the steps for making the letter m on the following line.

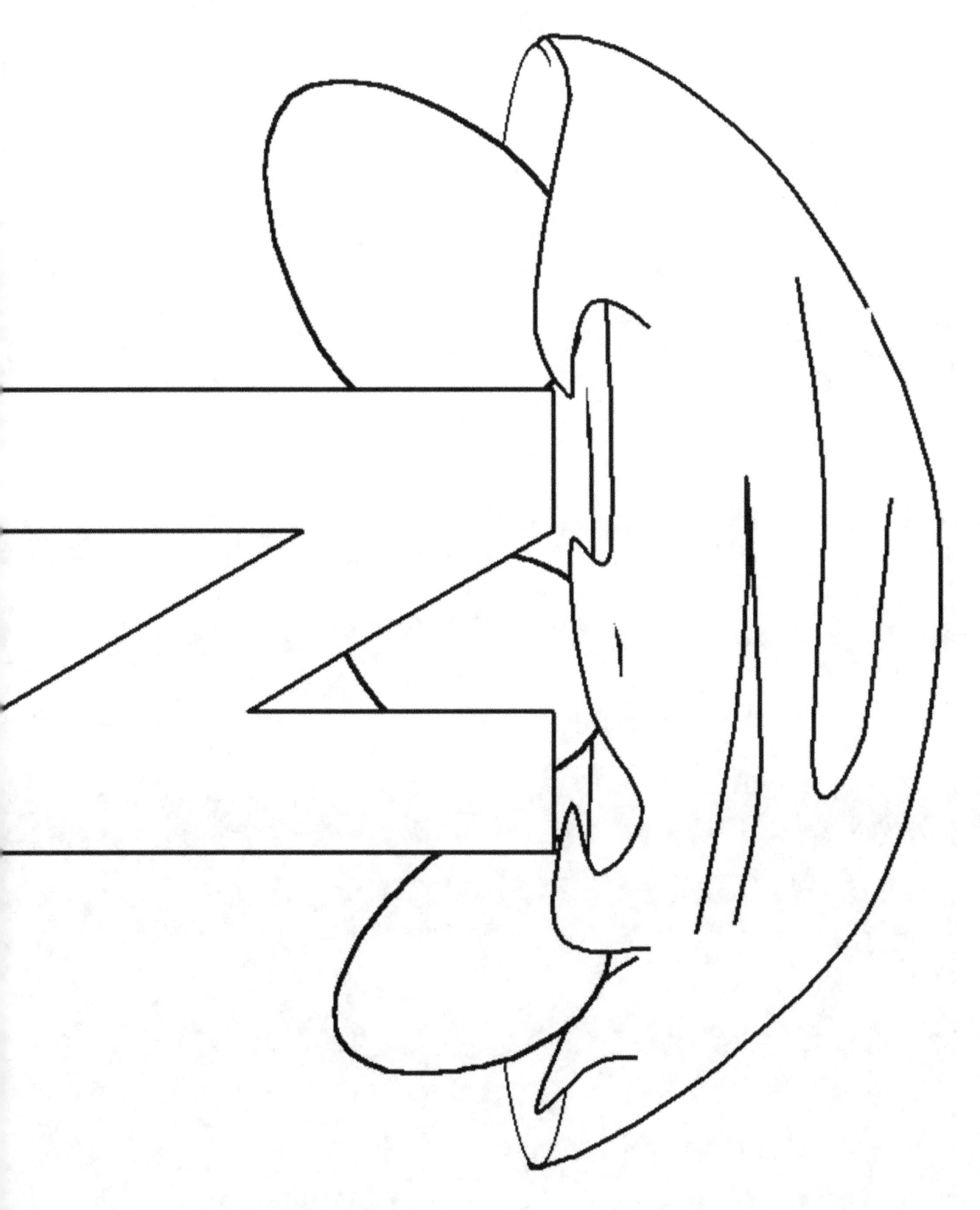

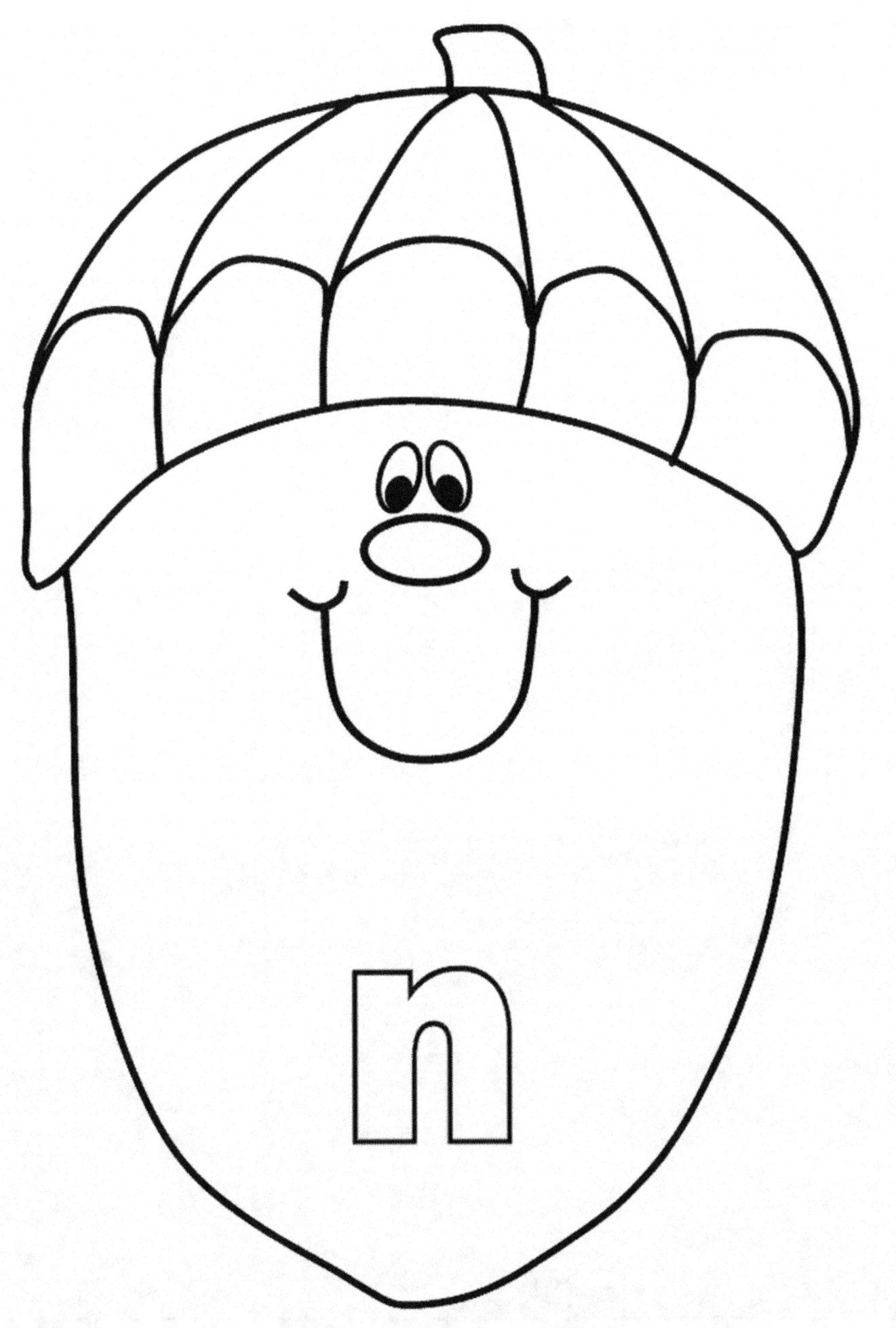

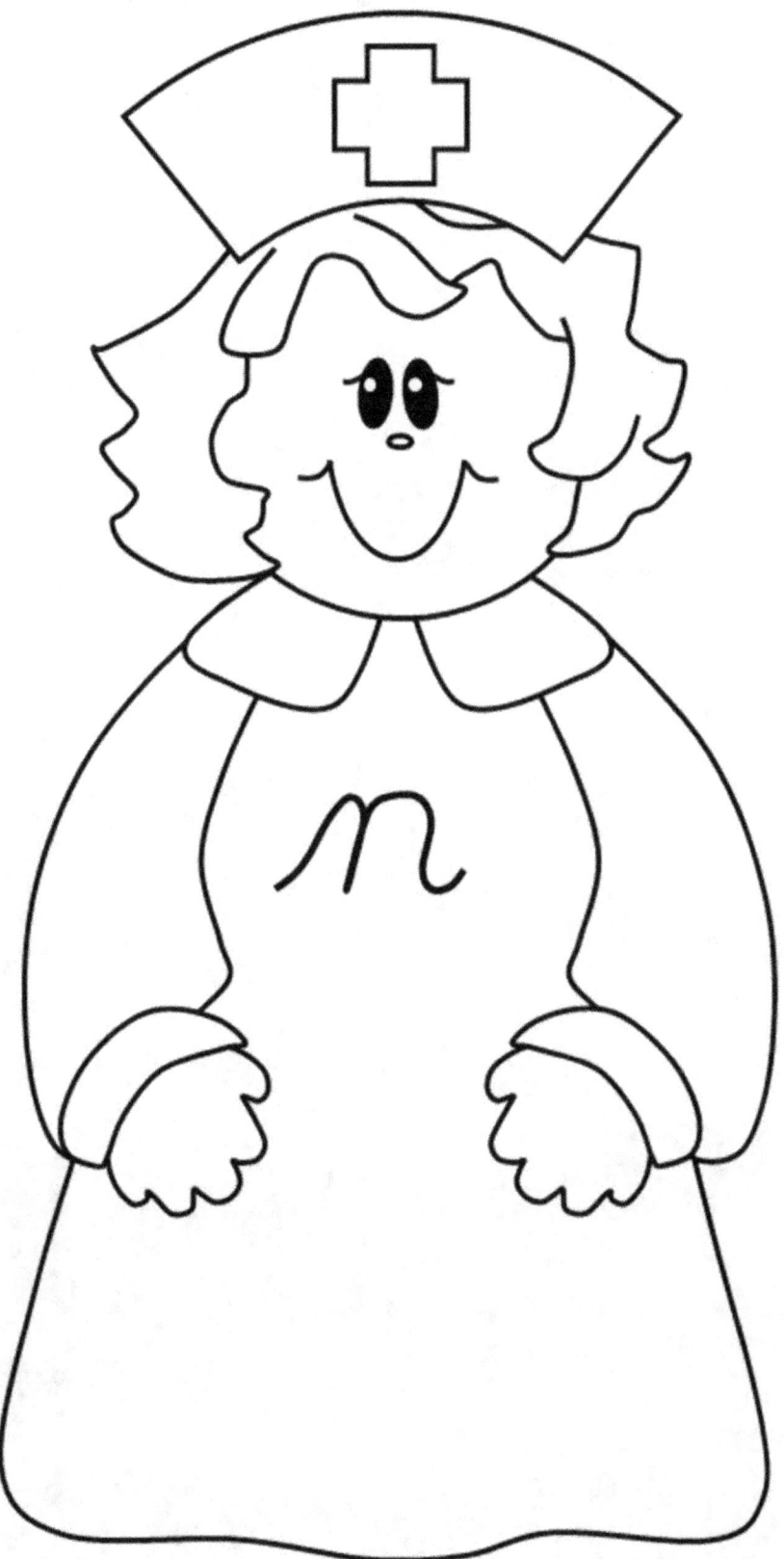

Trace the steps for making the letter n on the following line.

_____

⌐ ⌐ Л Л Л Л Л Л Л ЛЛ

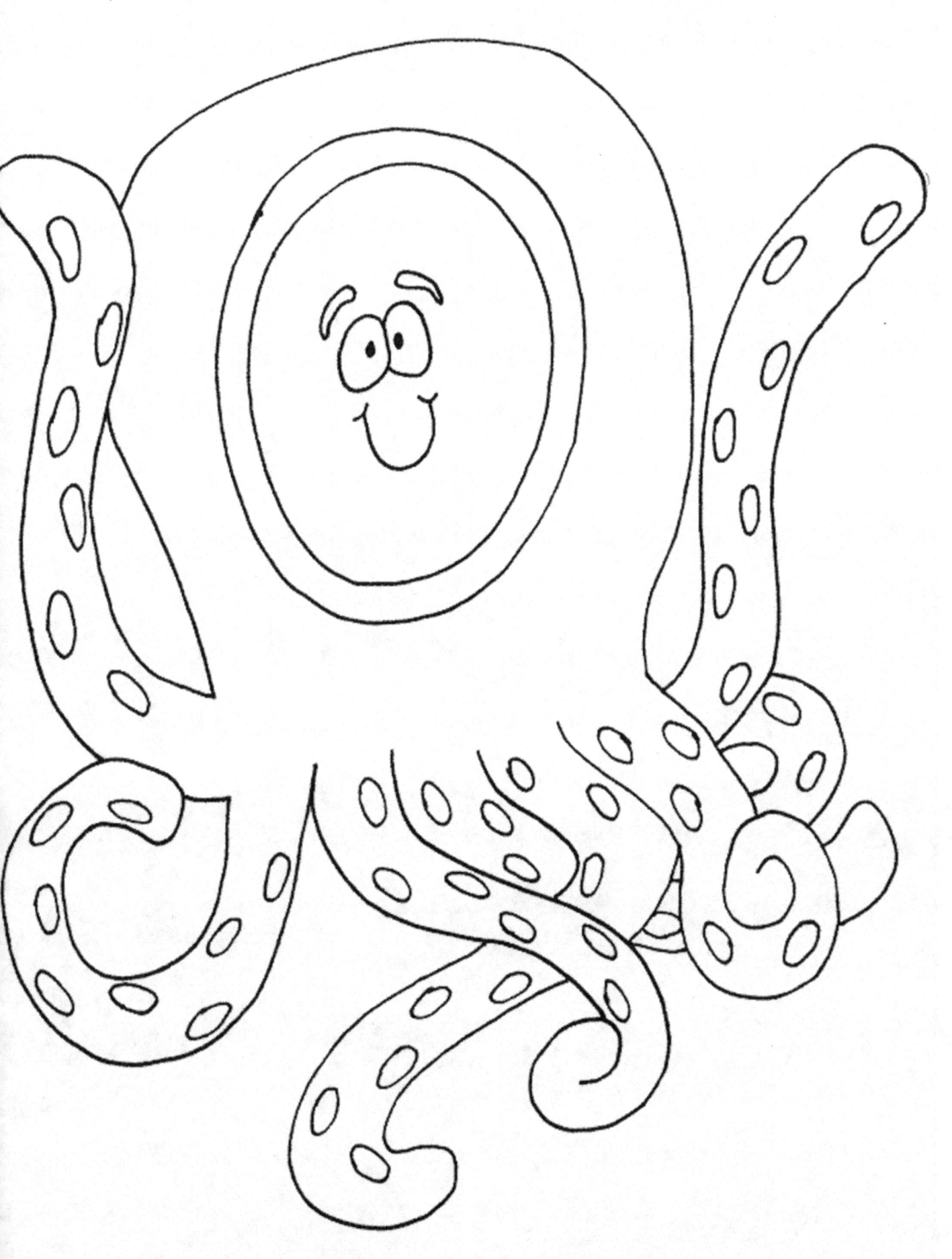

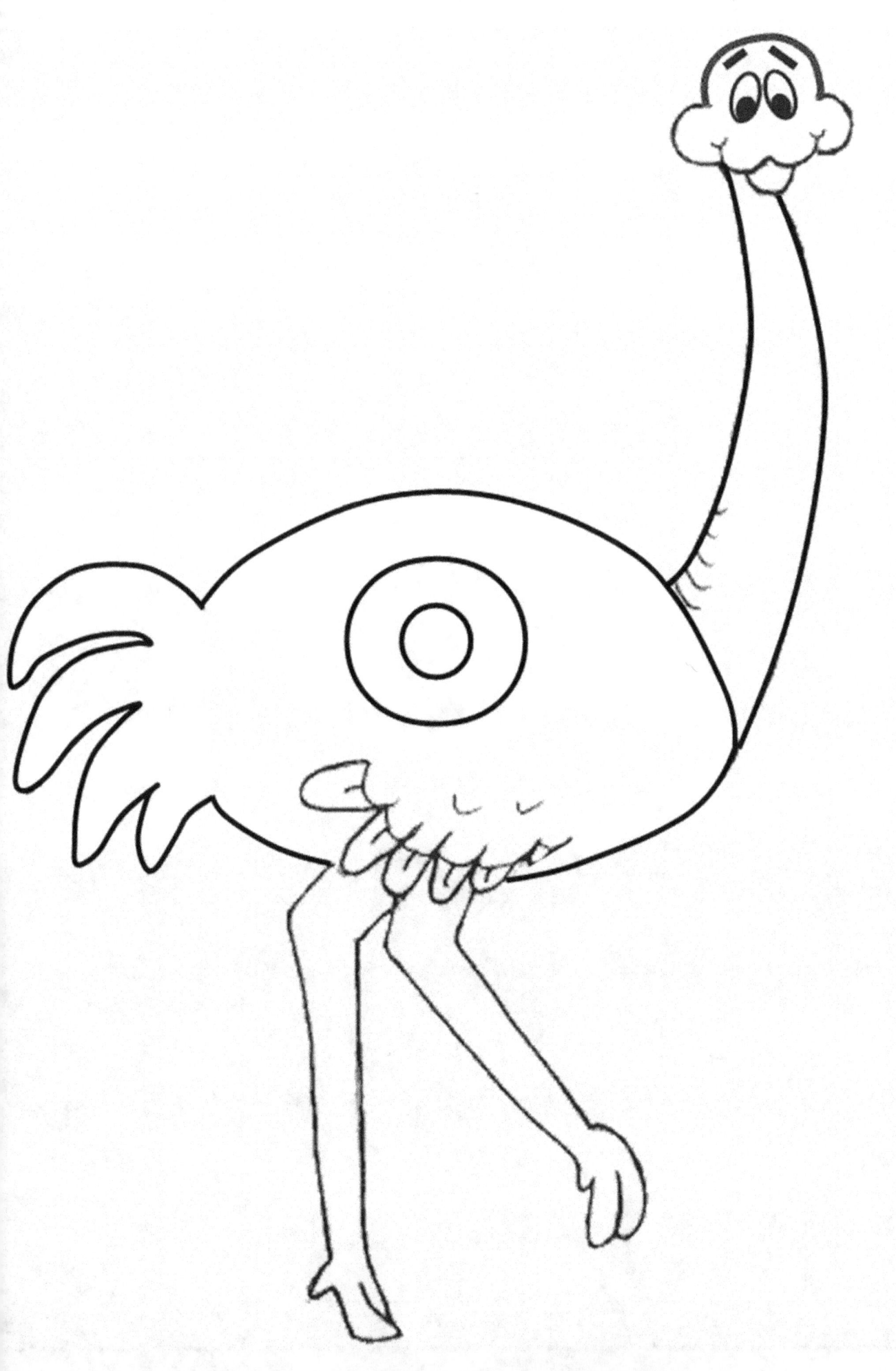

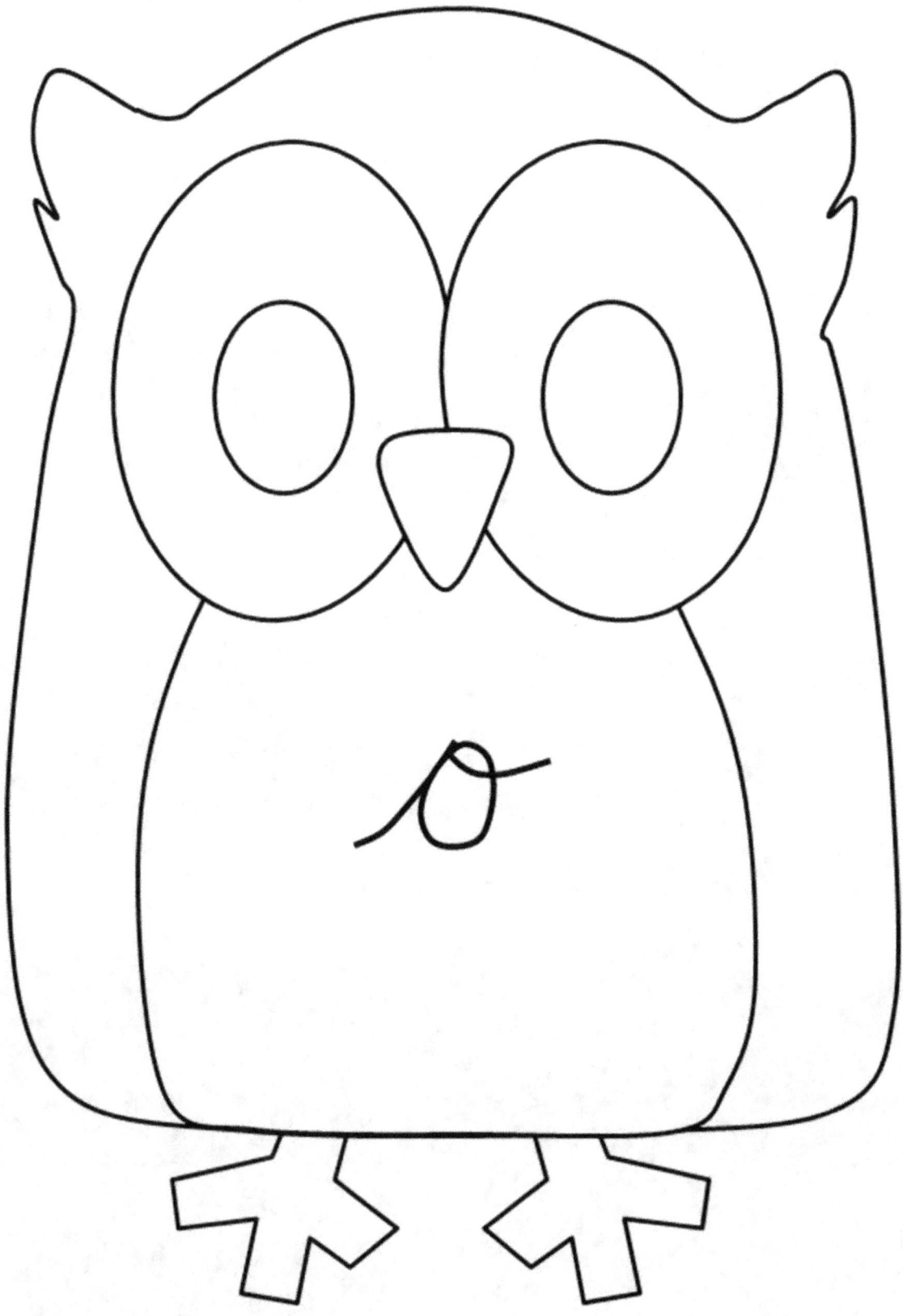

Trace the steps for making the letter o on the following line.

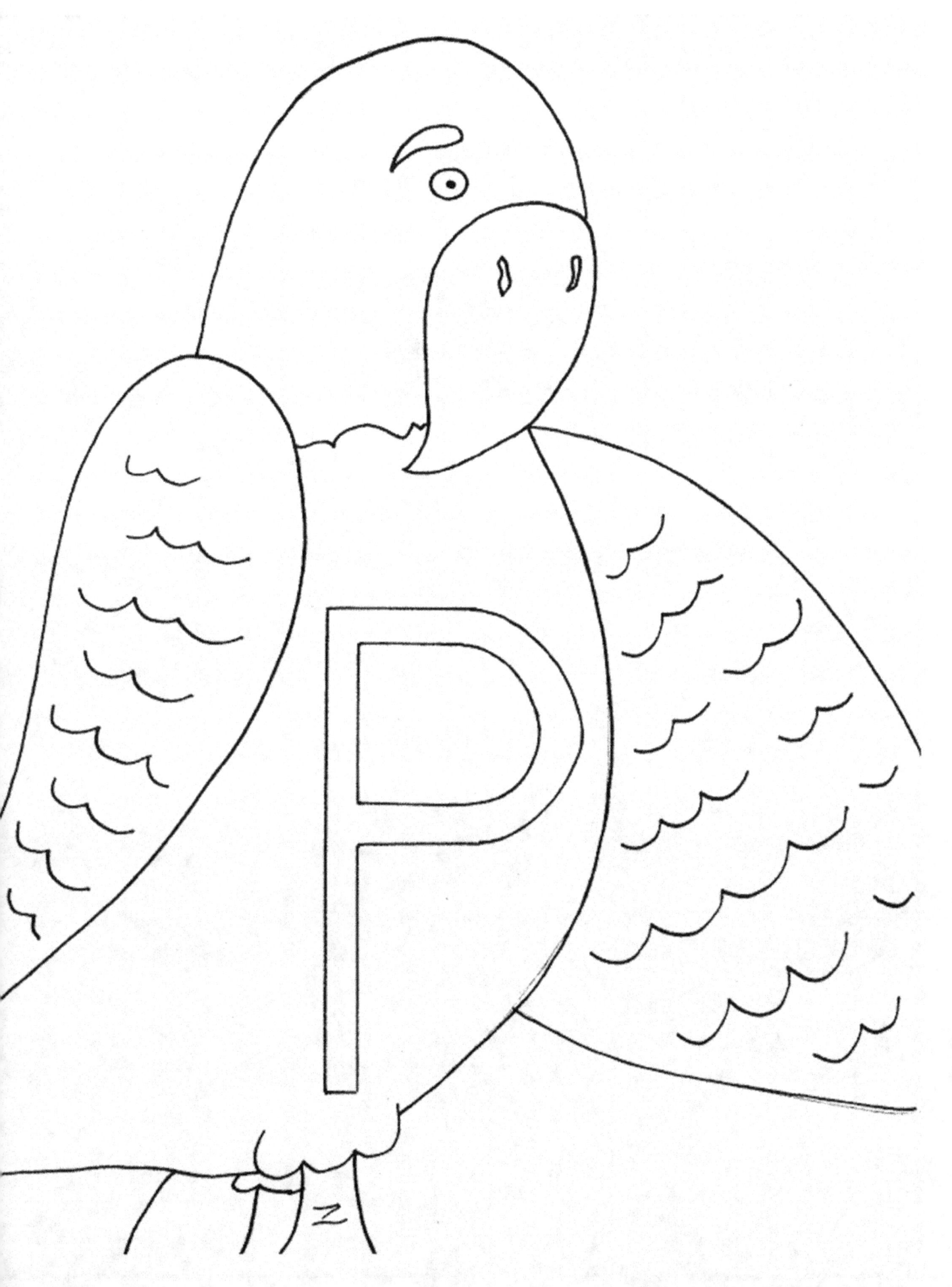

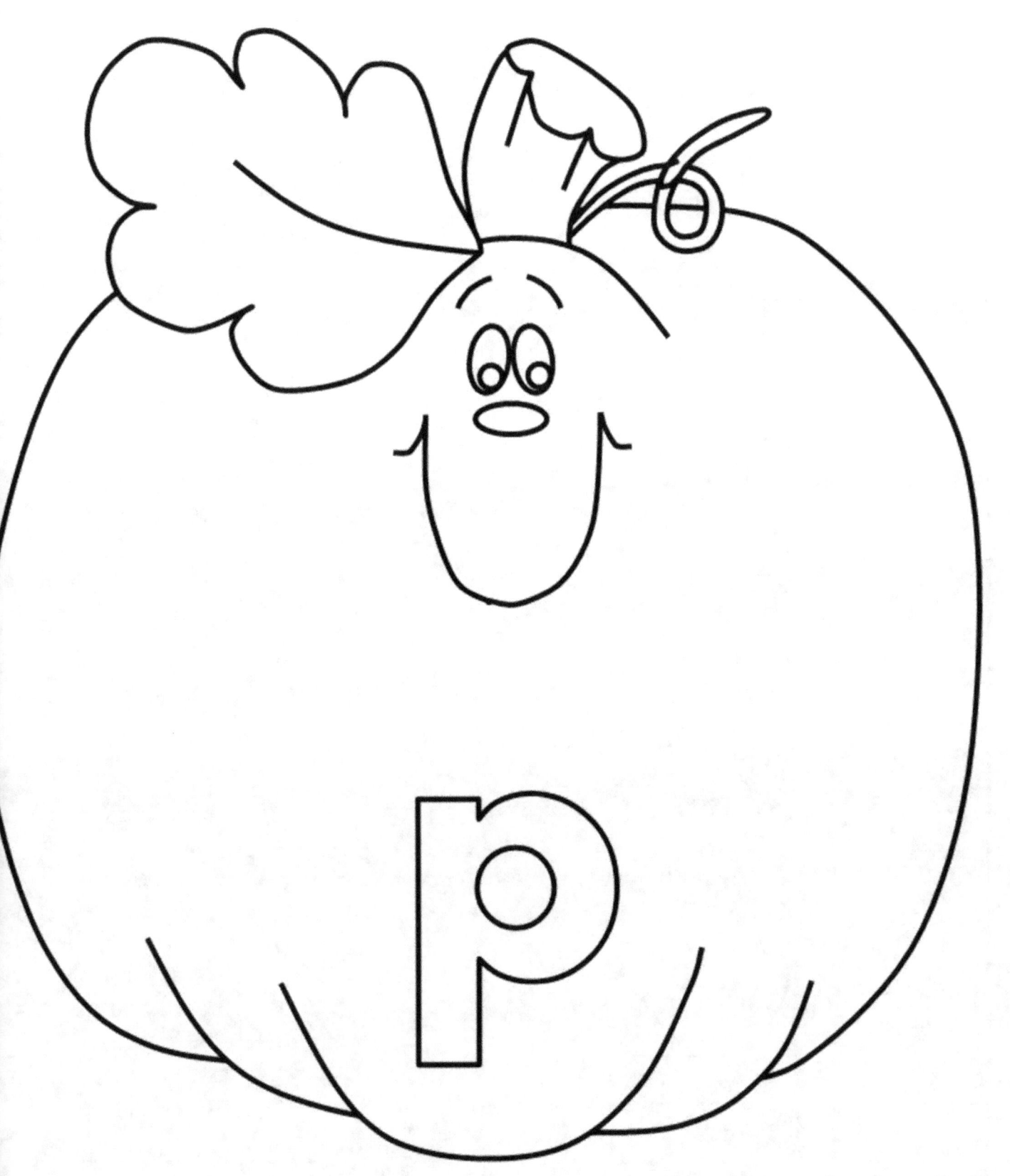

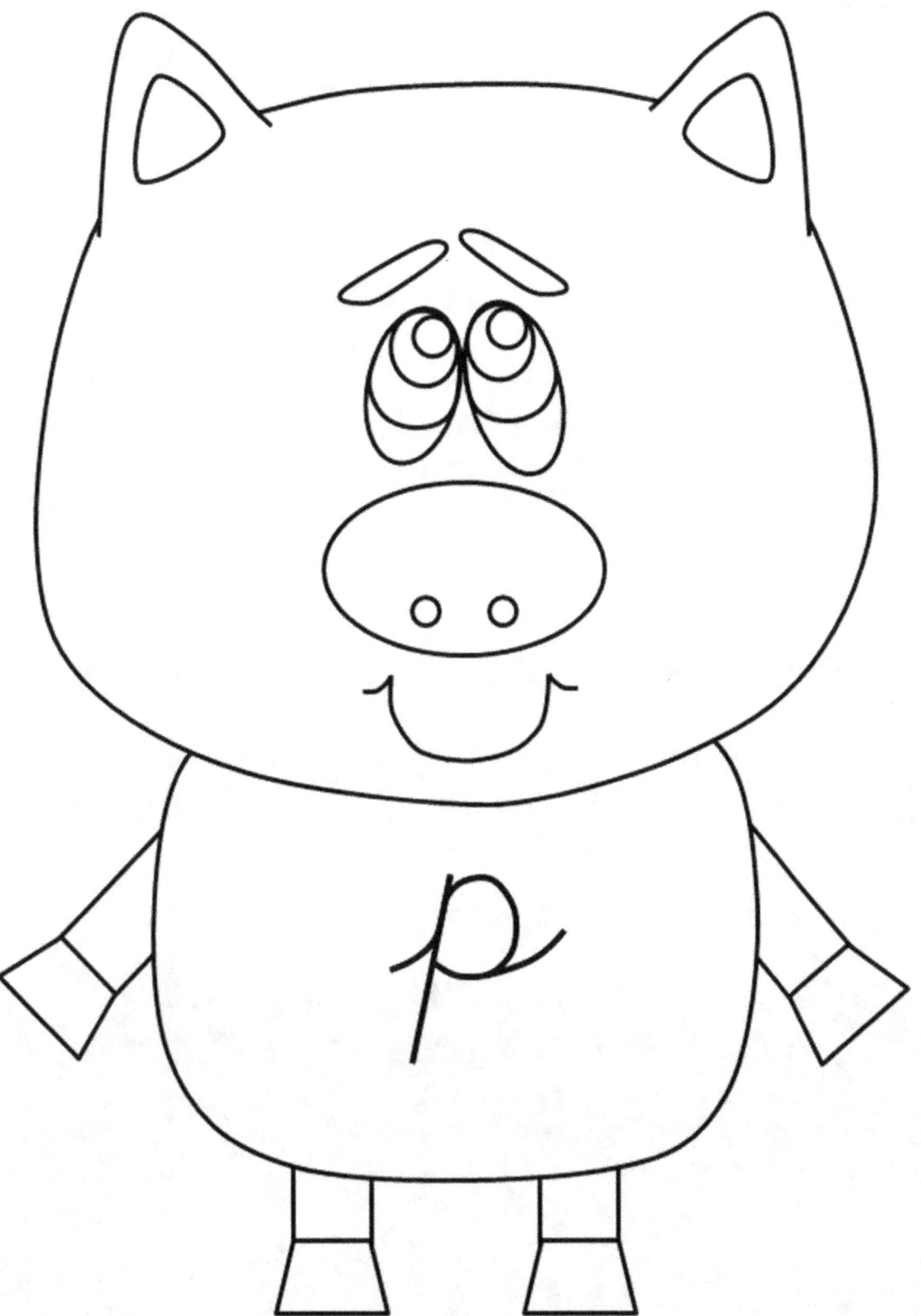

Trace the steps for making the letter p on the following line.

$\overline{}$

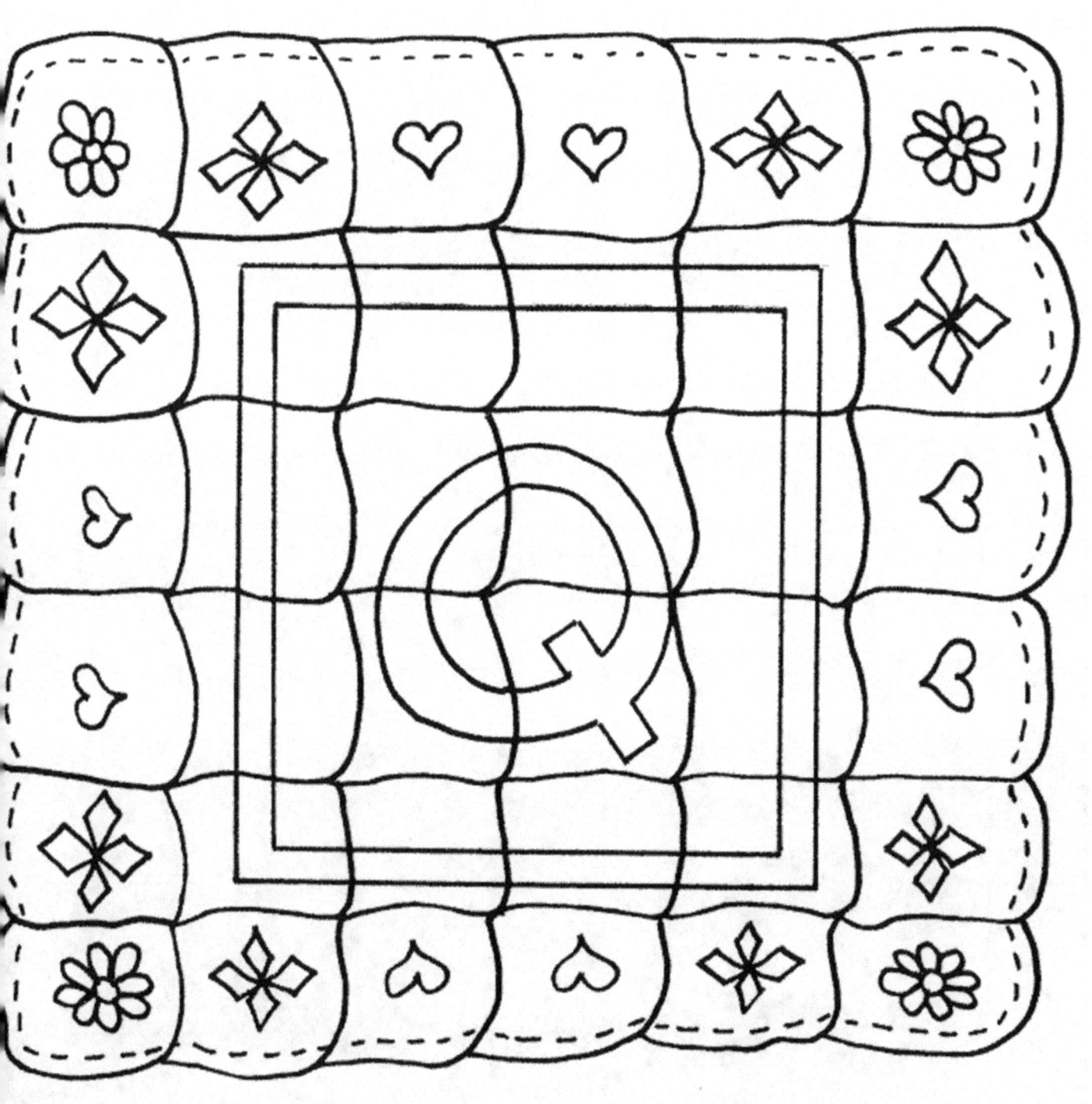

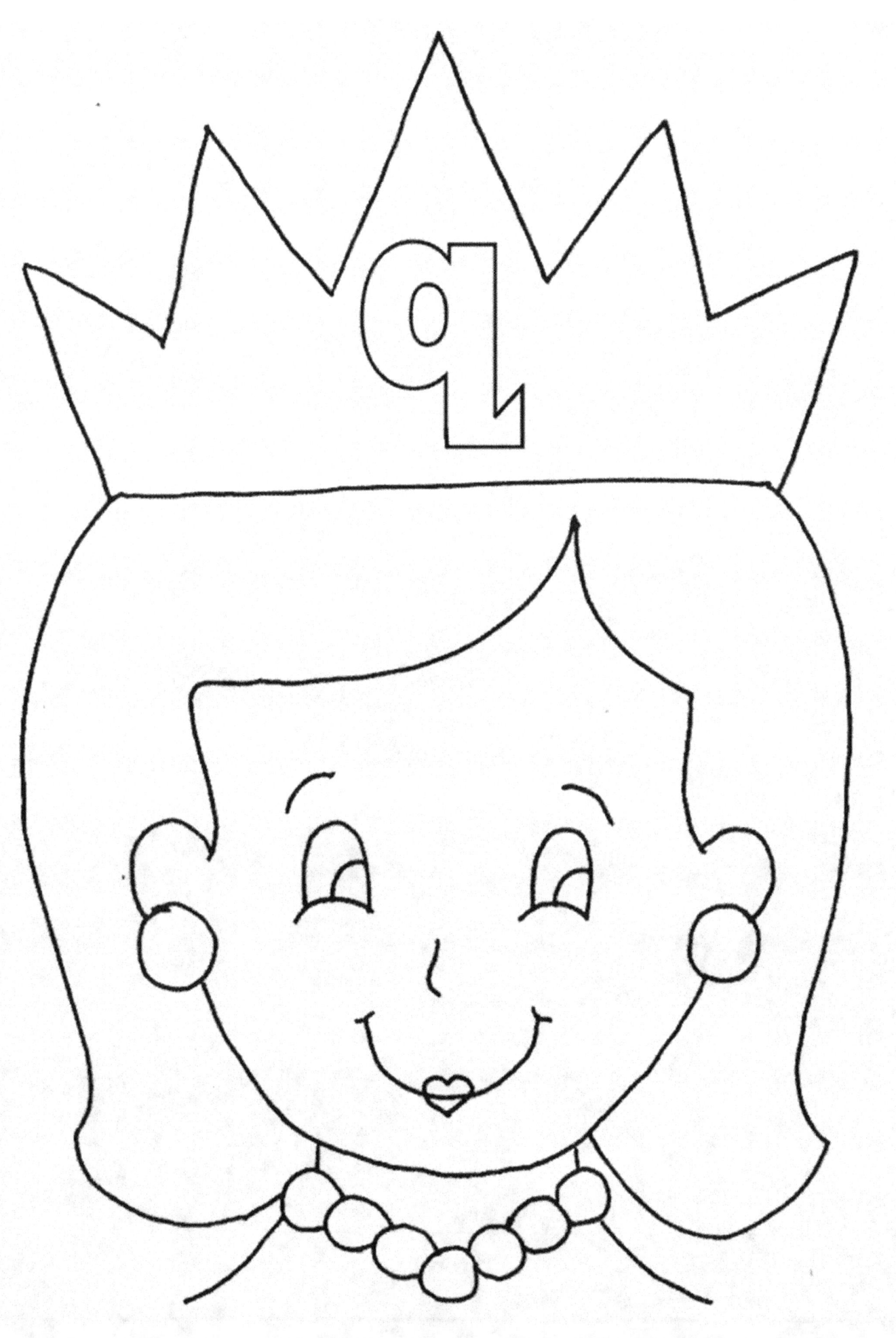

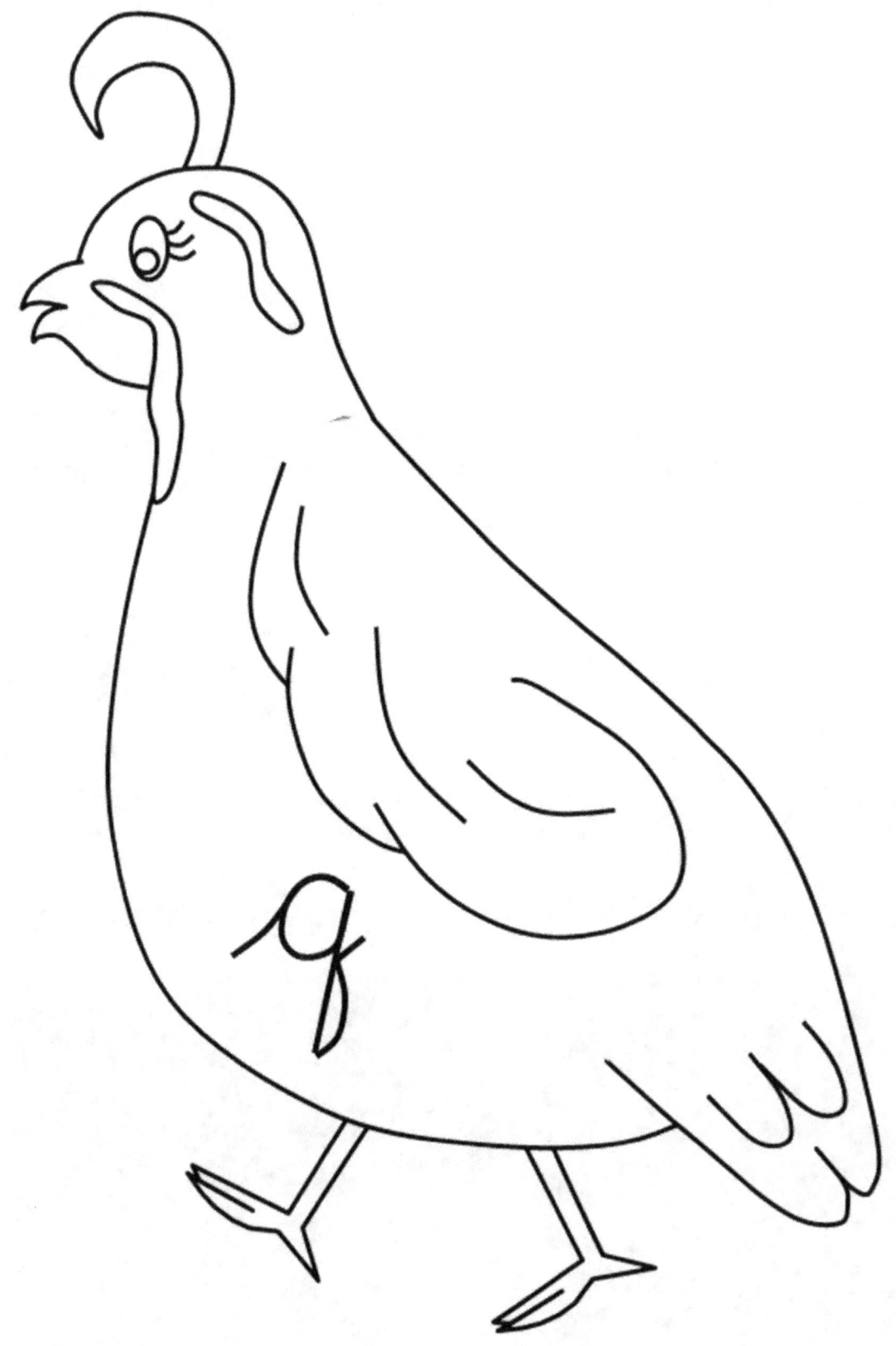

Trace the steps for making the letter q on the following line.

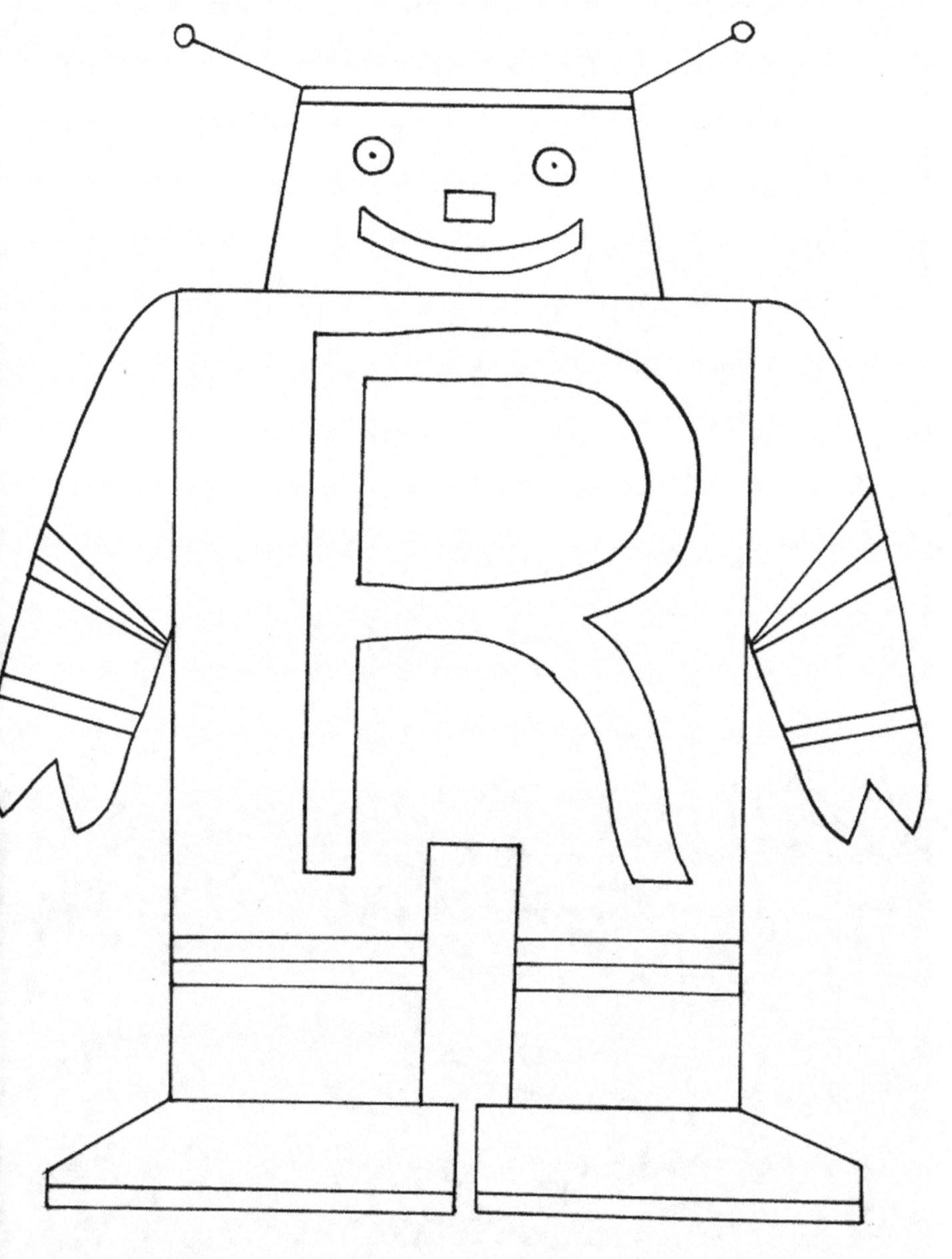

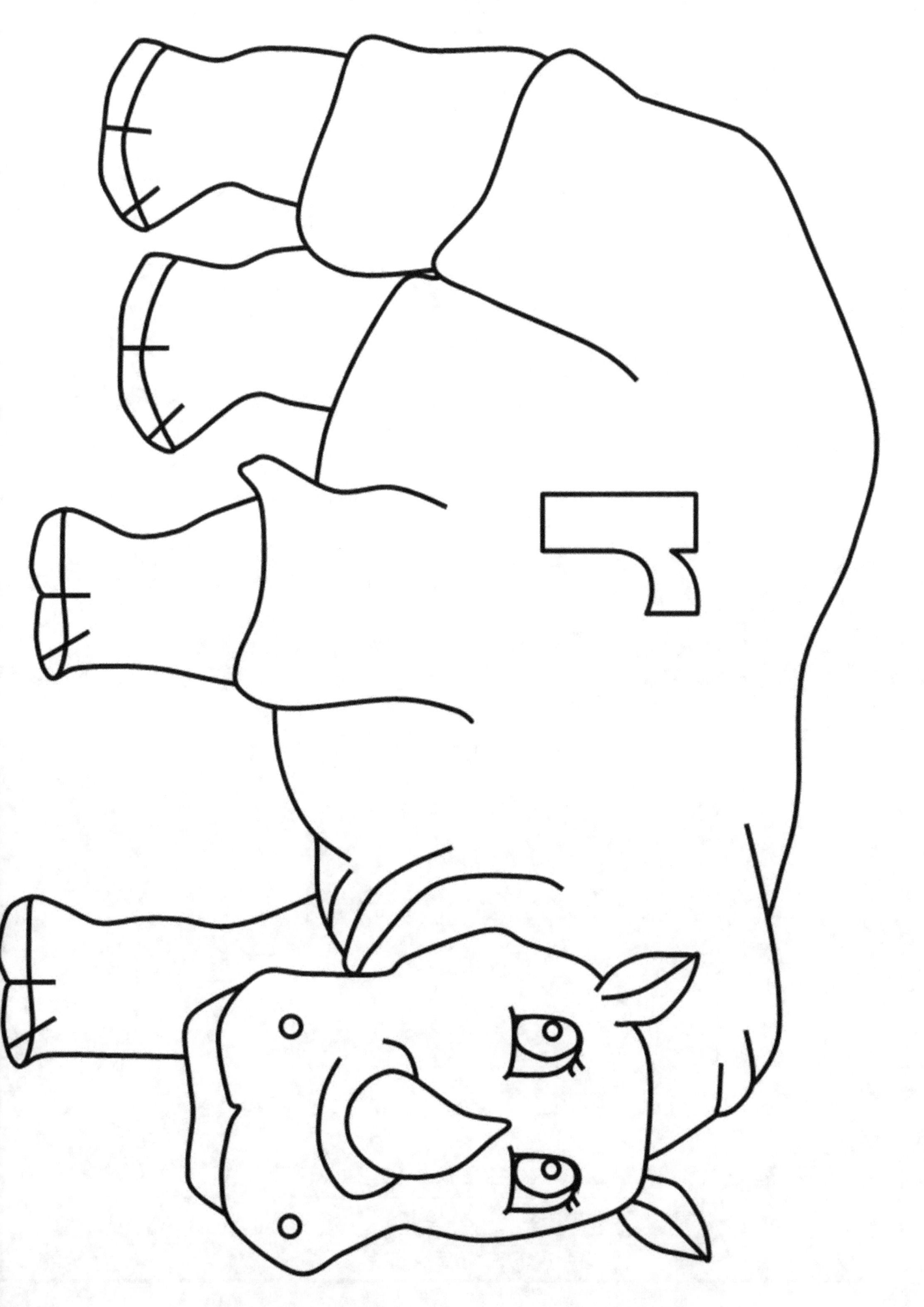

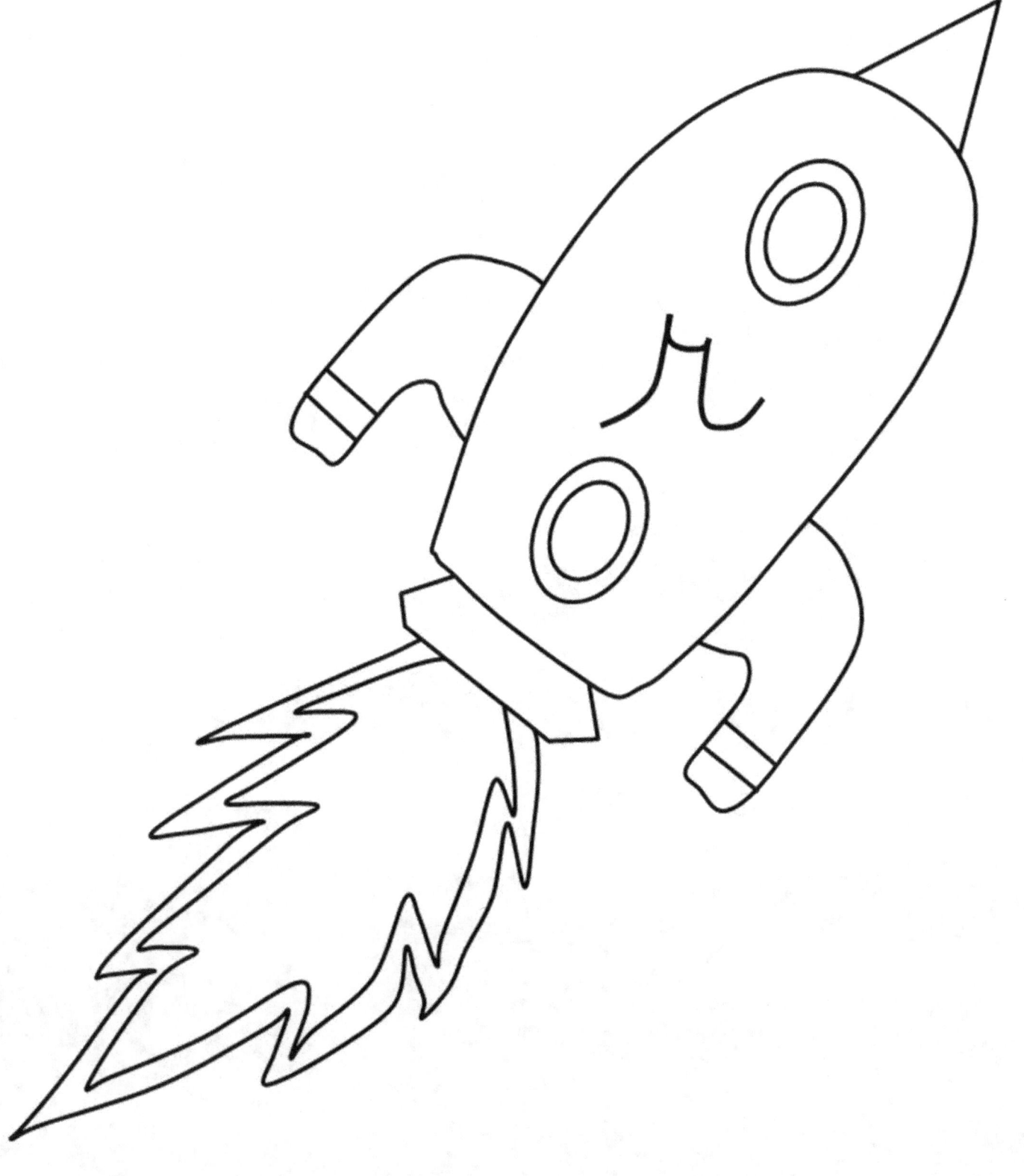

Trace the steps for making the letter r on the following line.

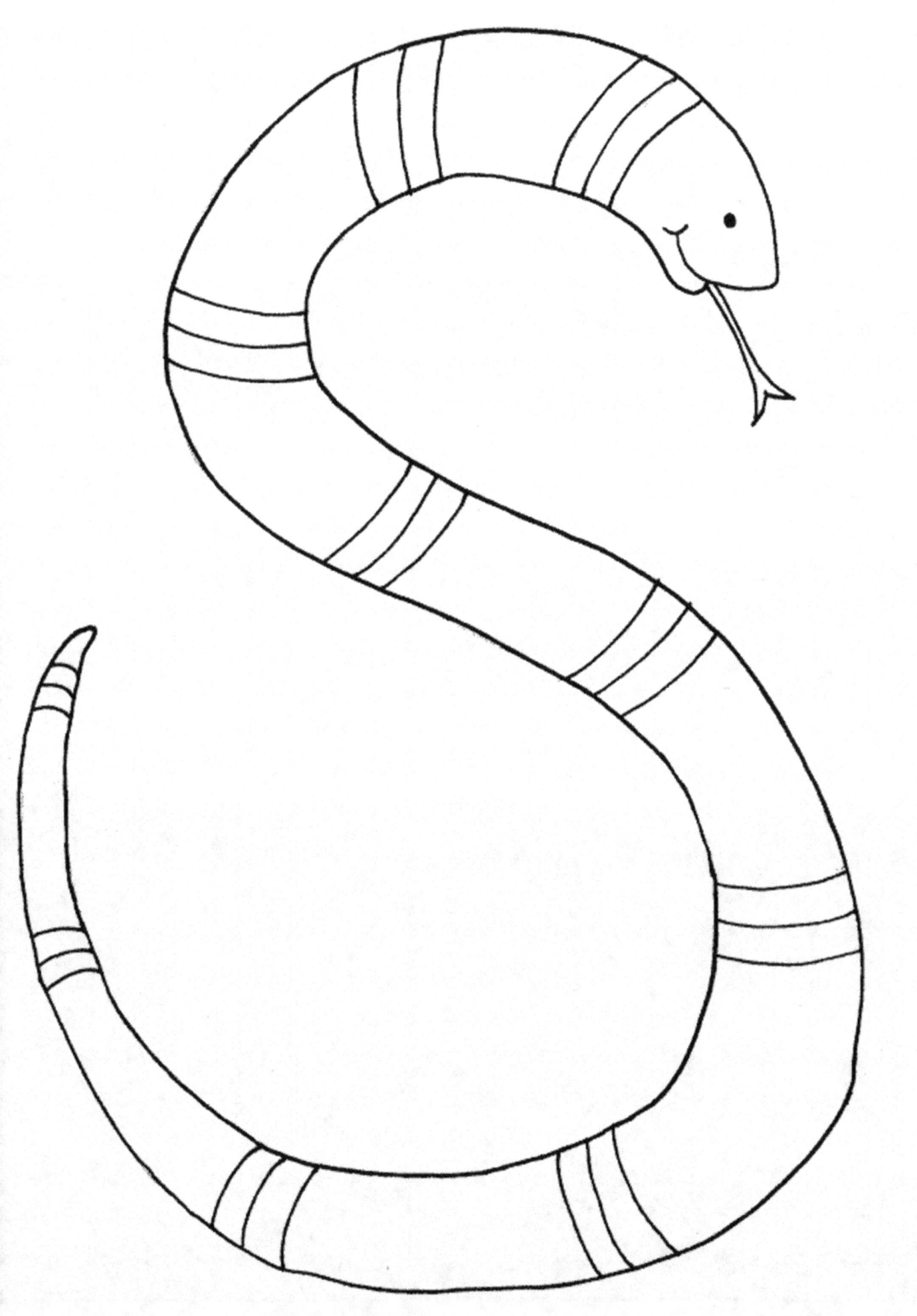

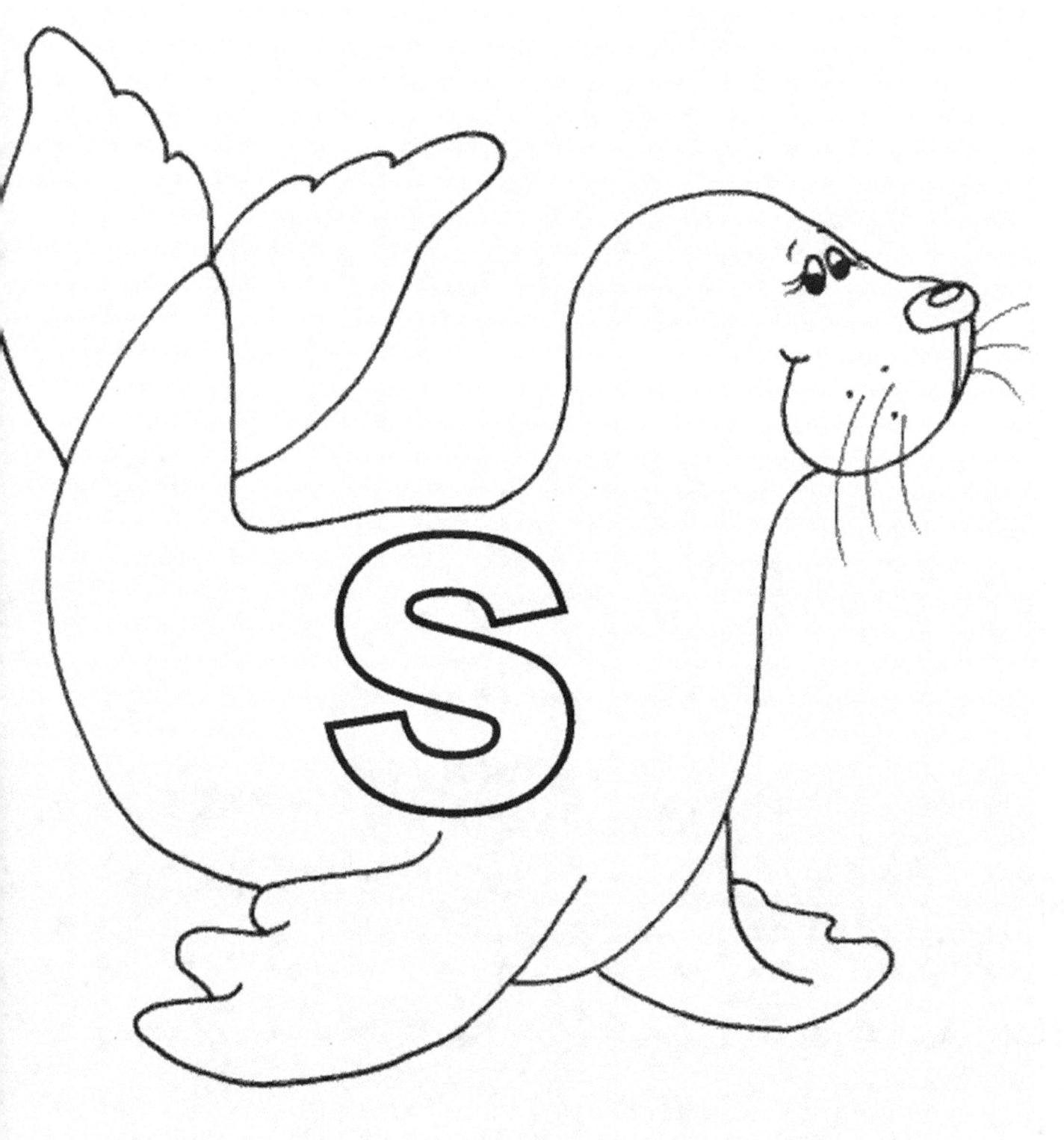

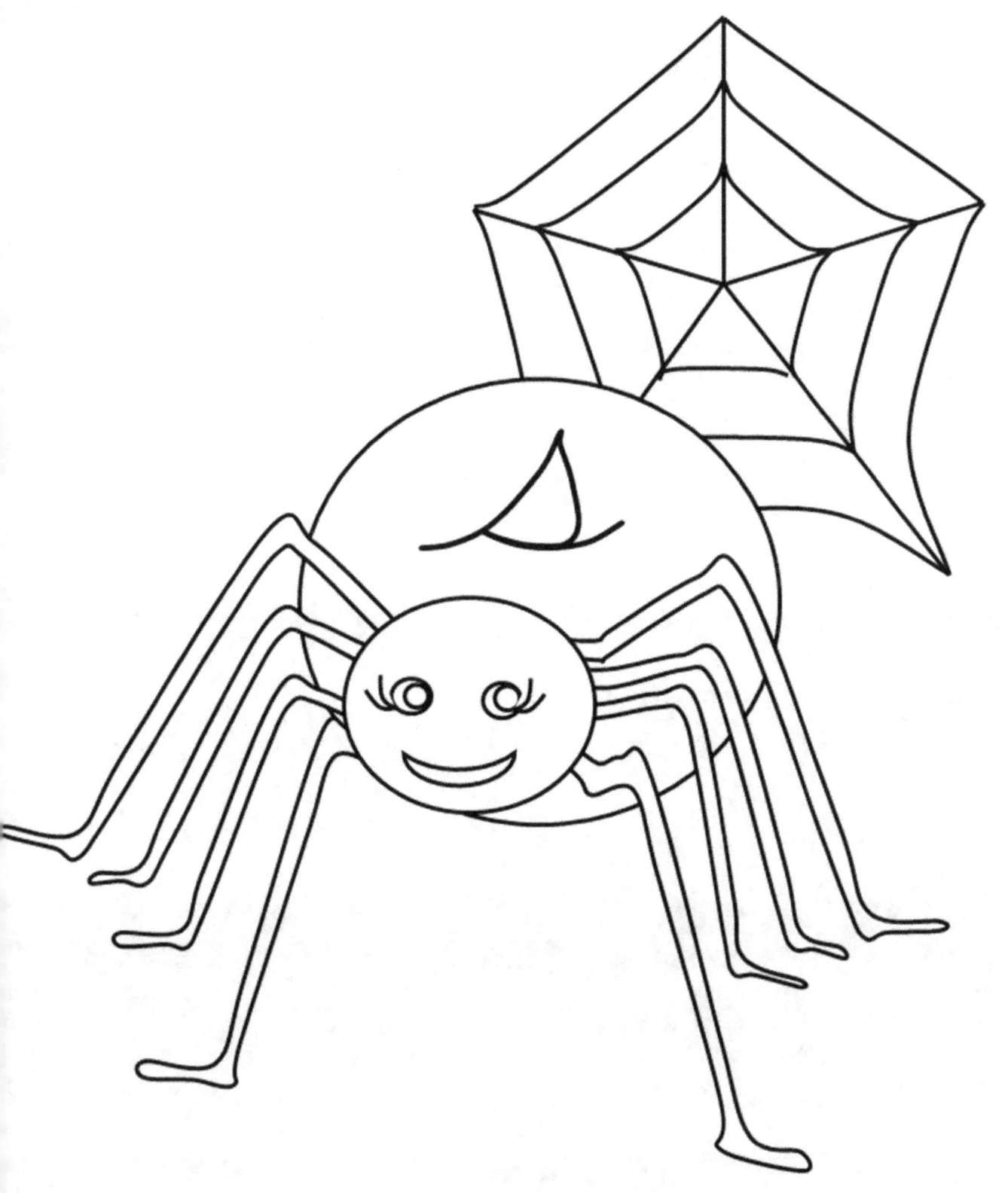

Trace the steps for making the letter s on the following line.

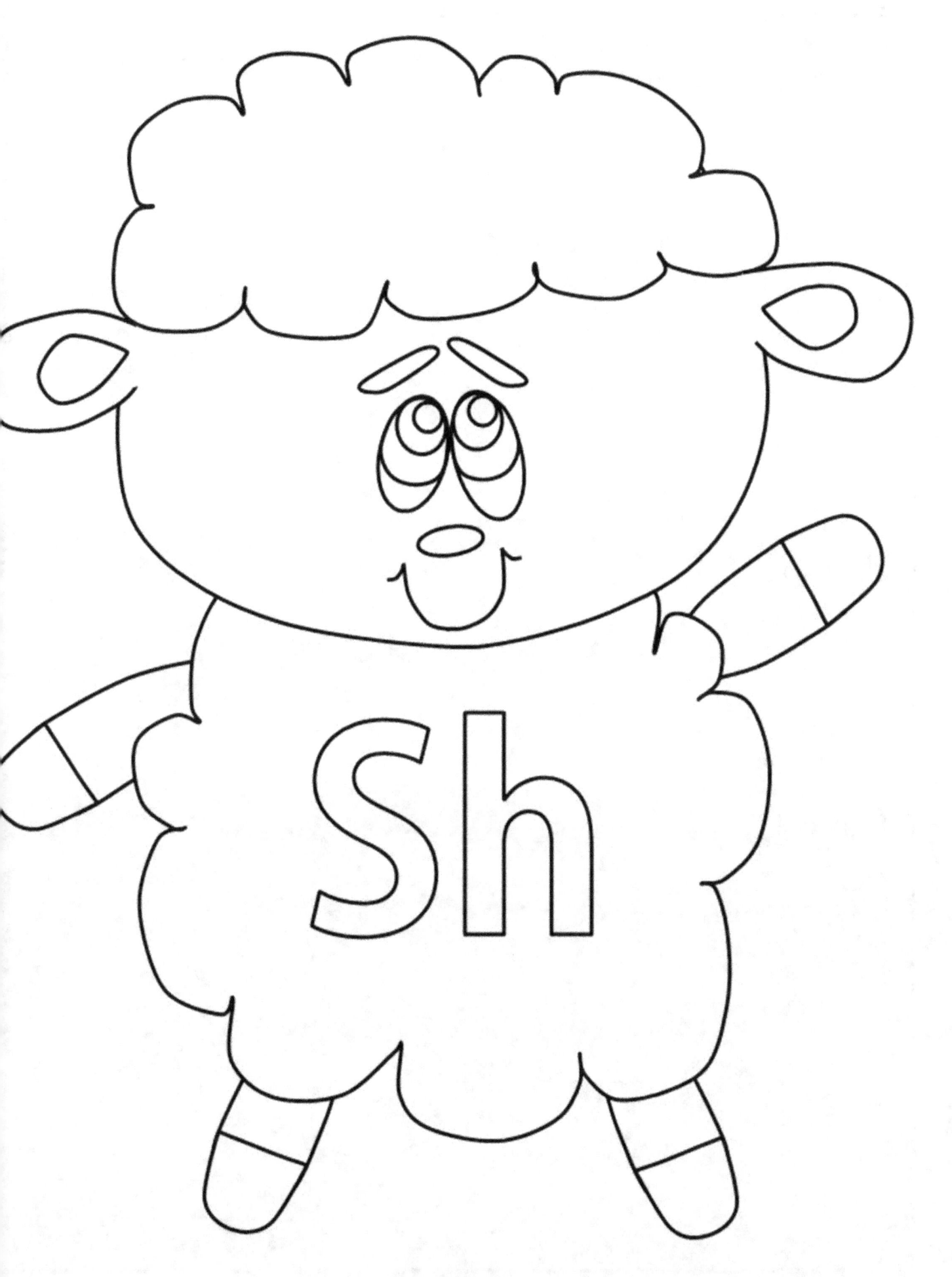

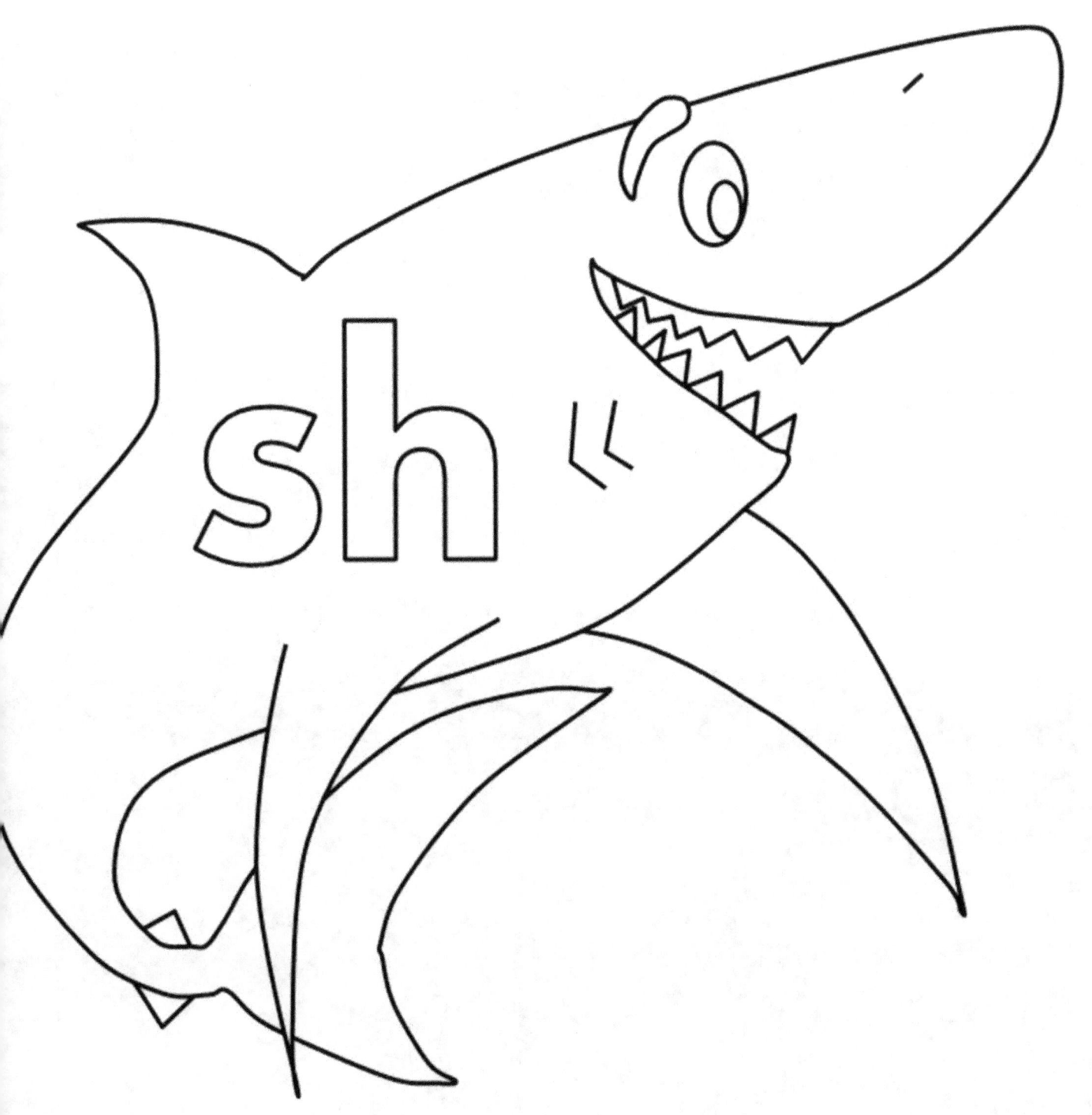

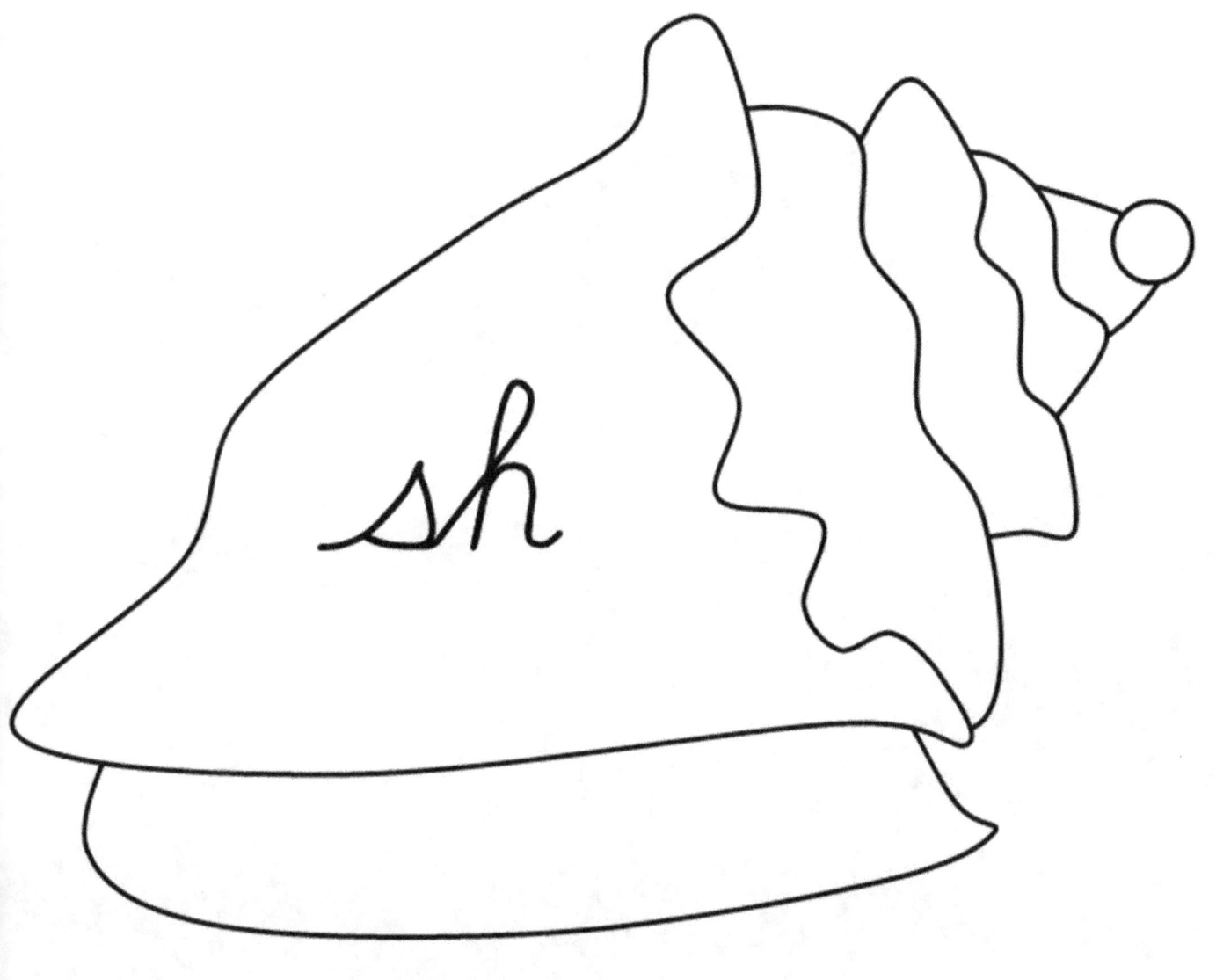

Trace the steps for making the letter sh on the following line.

_sh_ _sh_ _sh_ _sh_ _sh_

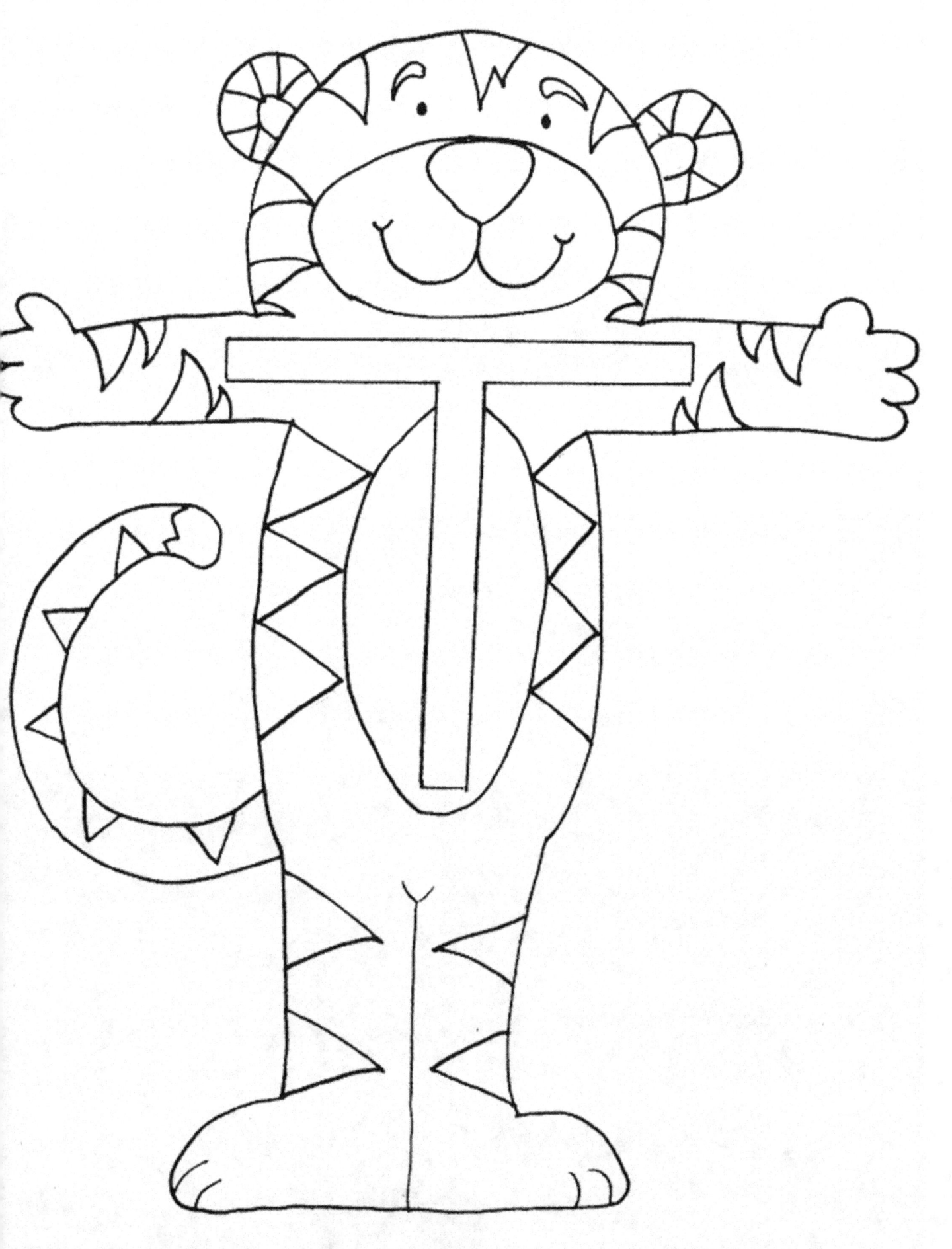

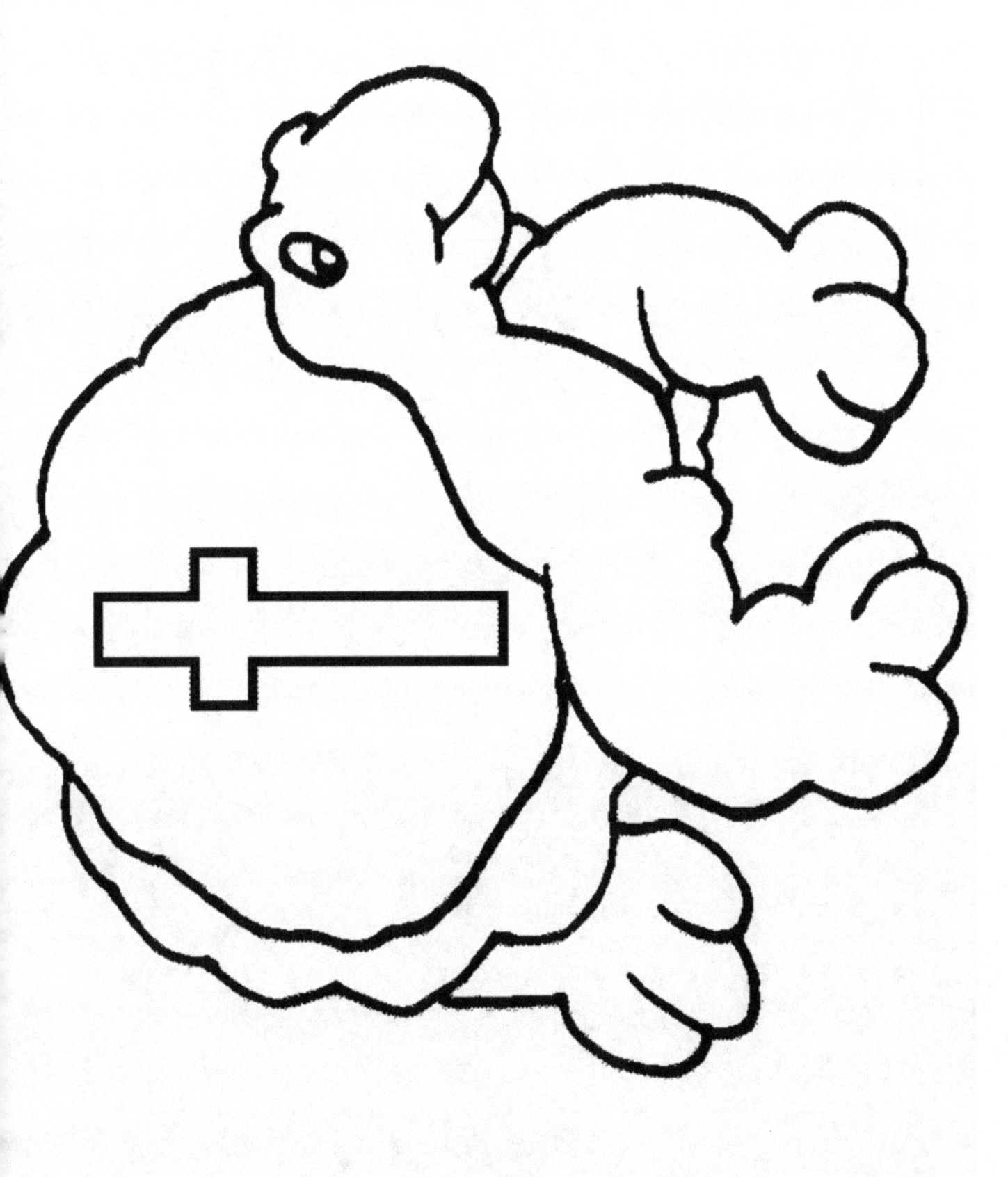

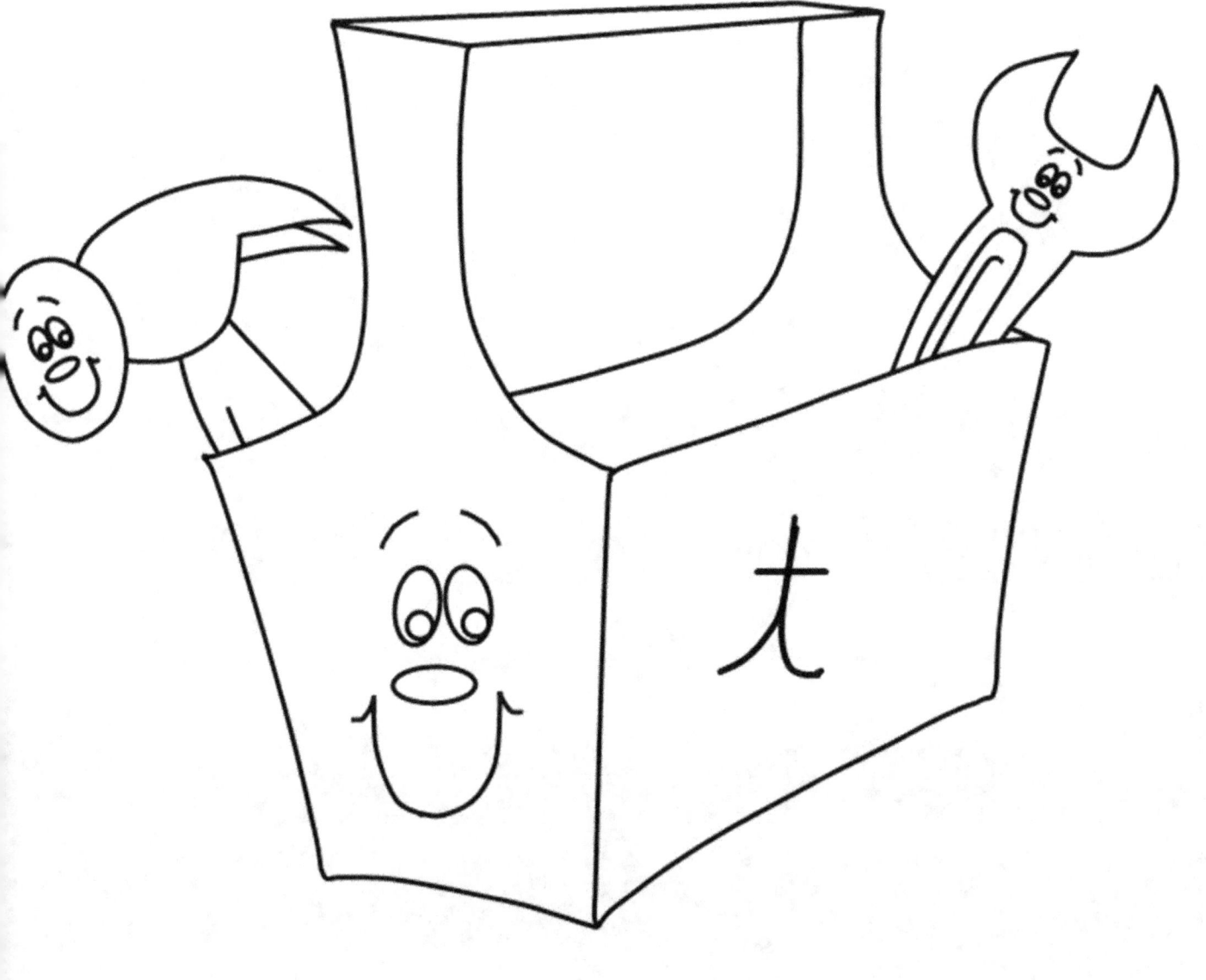

Trace the steps for making the letter t on the following line.

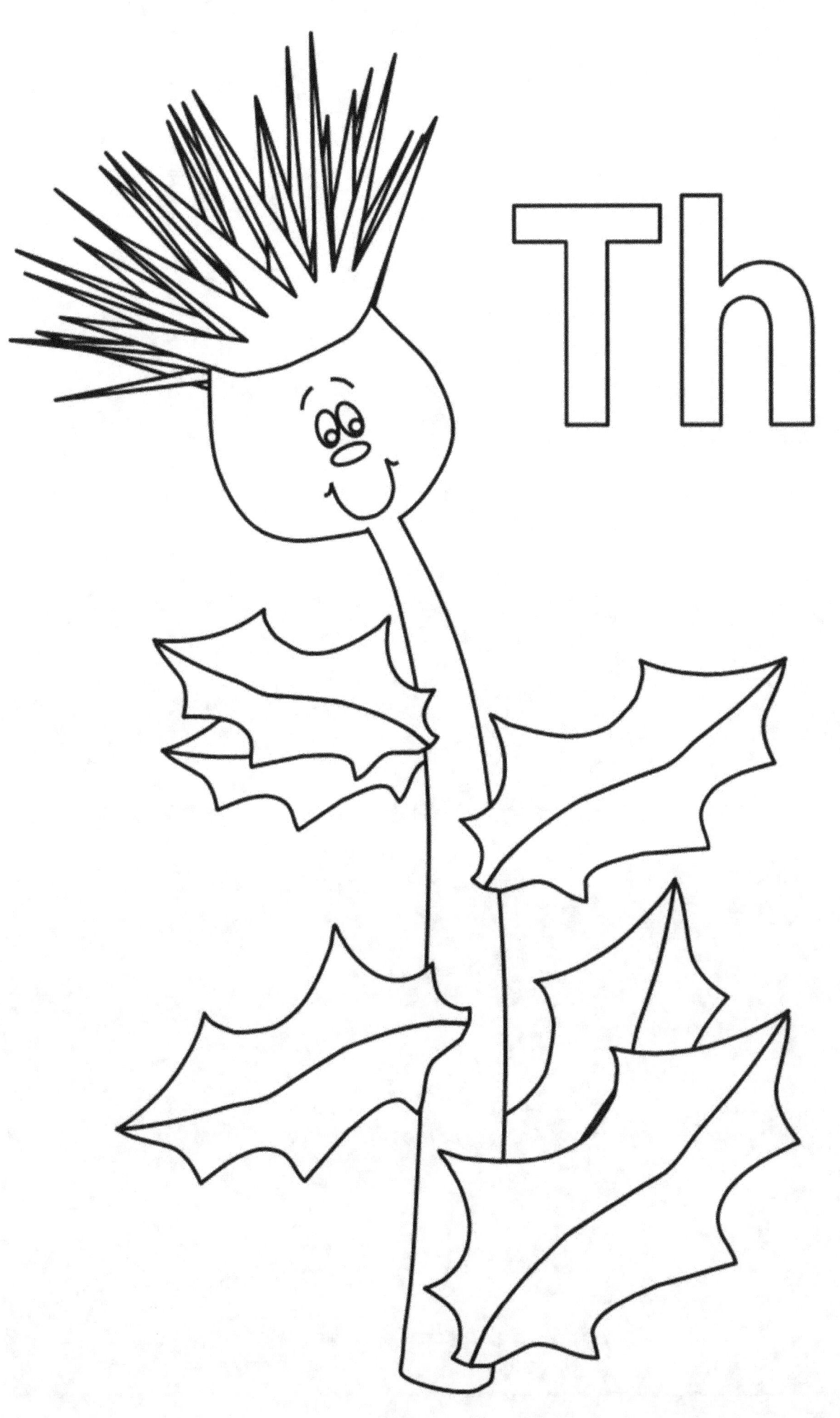

Th

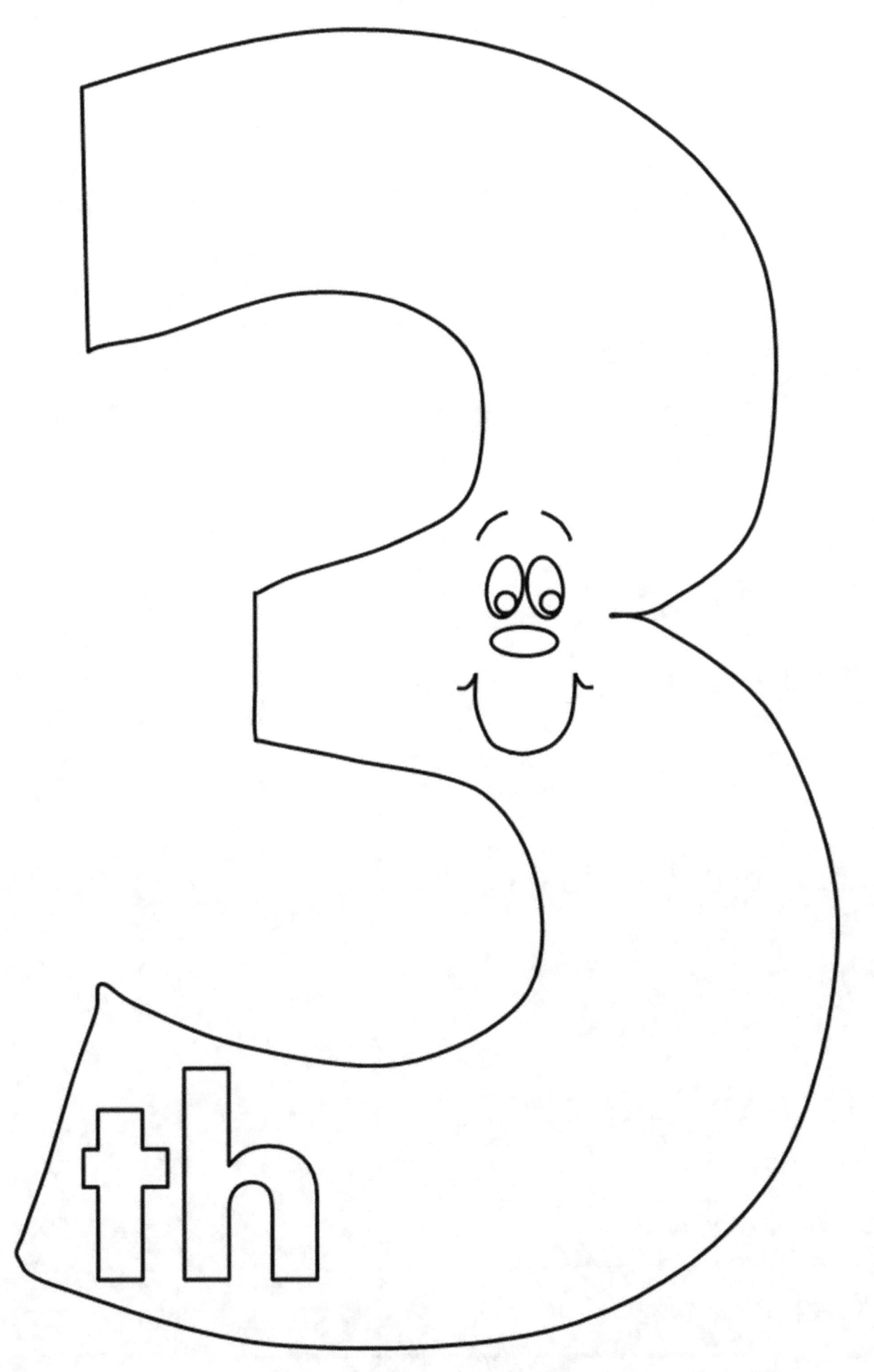

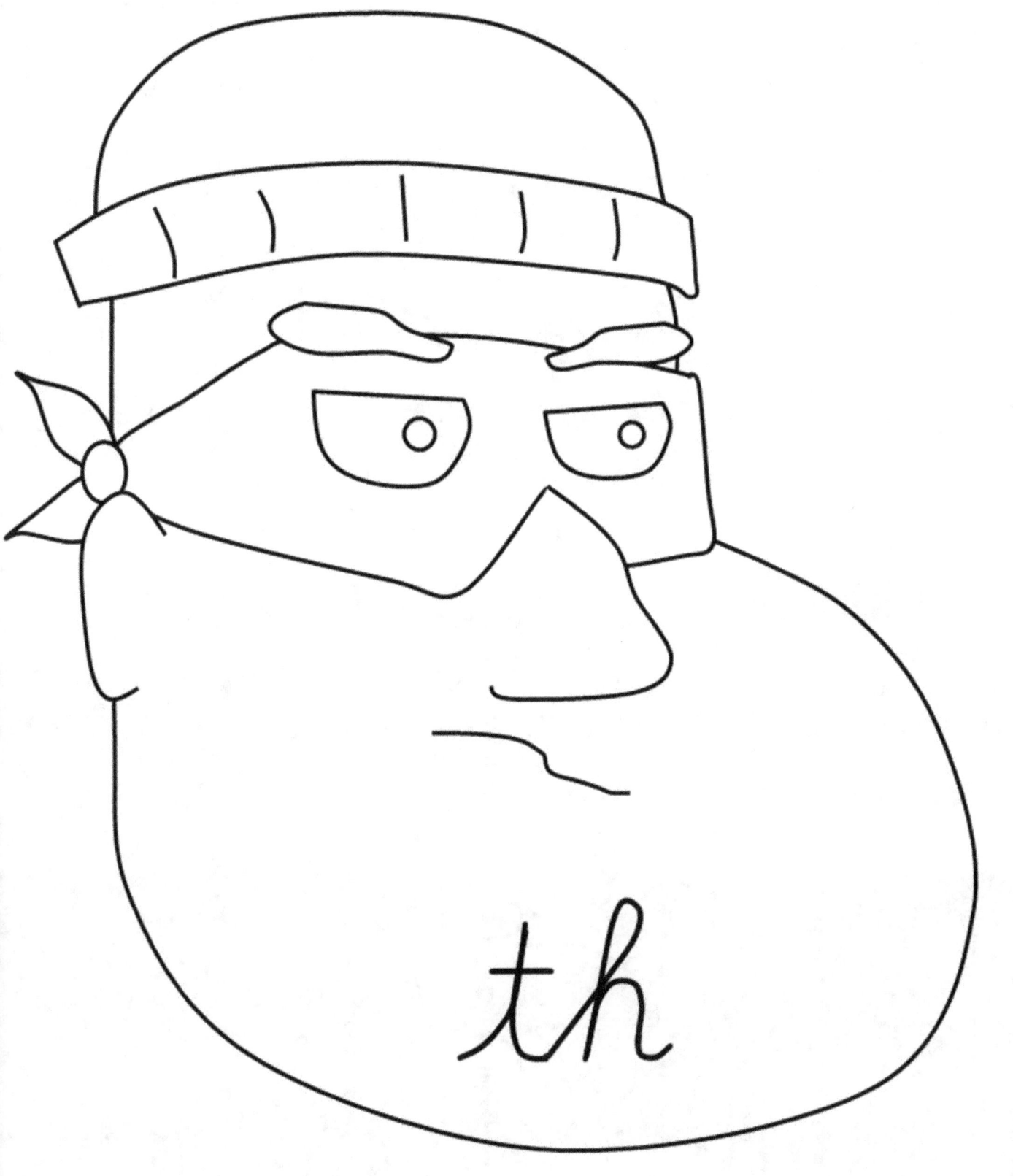

Trace the steps for making the letter th on the following line.

t *h* *th* *th* *th* *th*

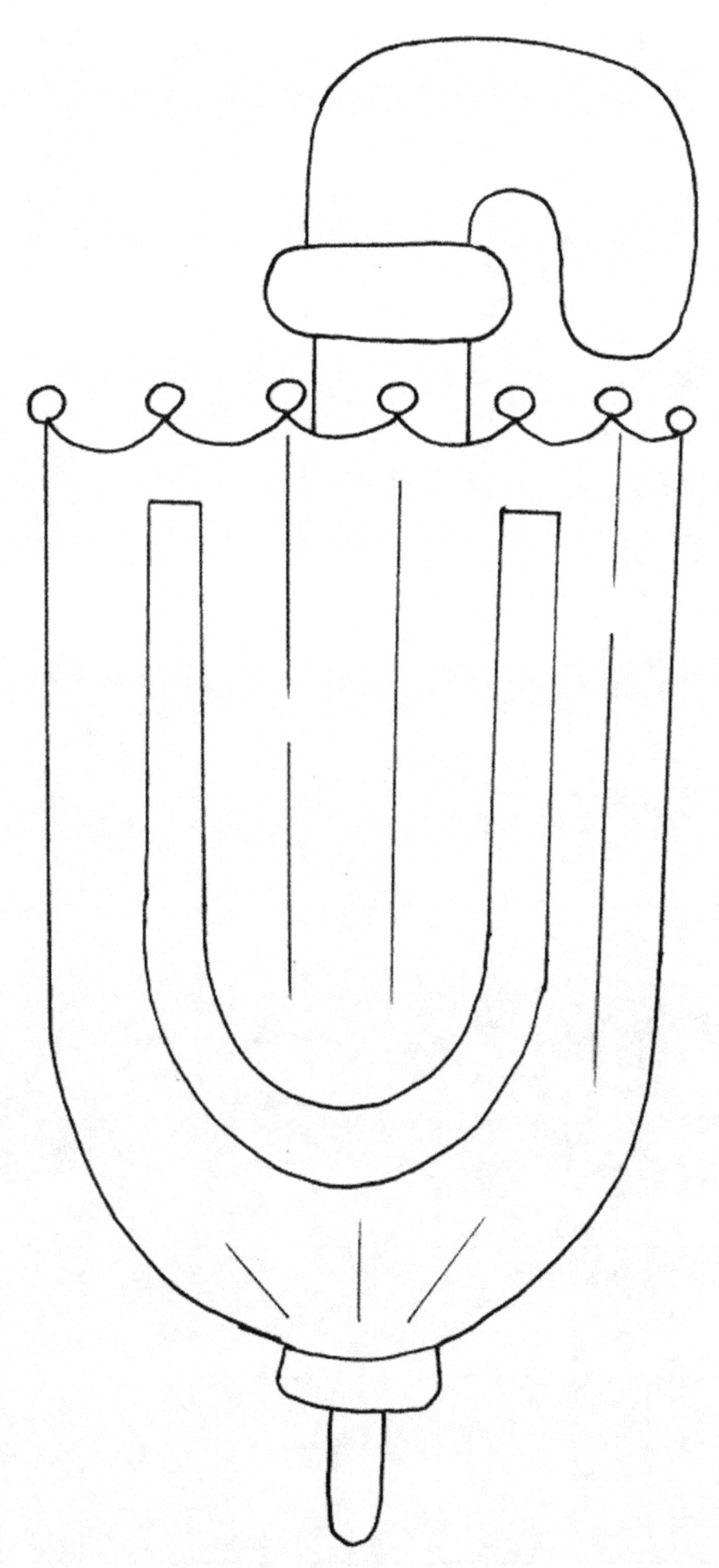

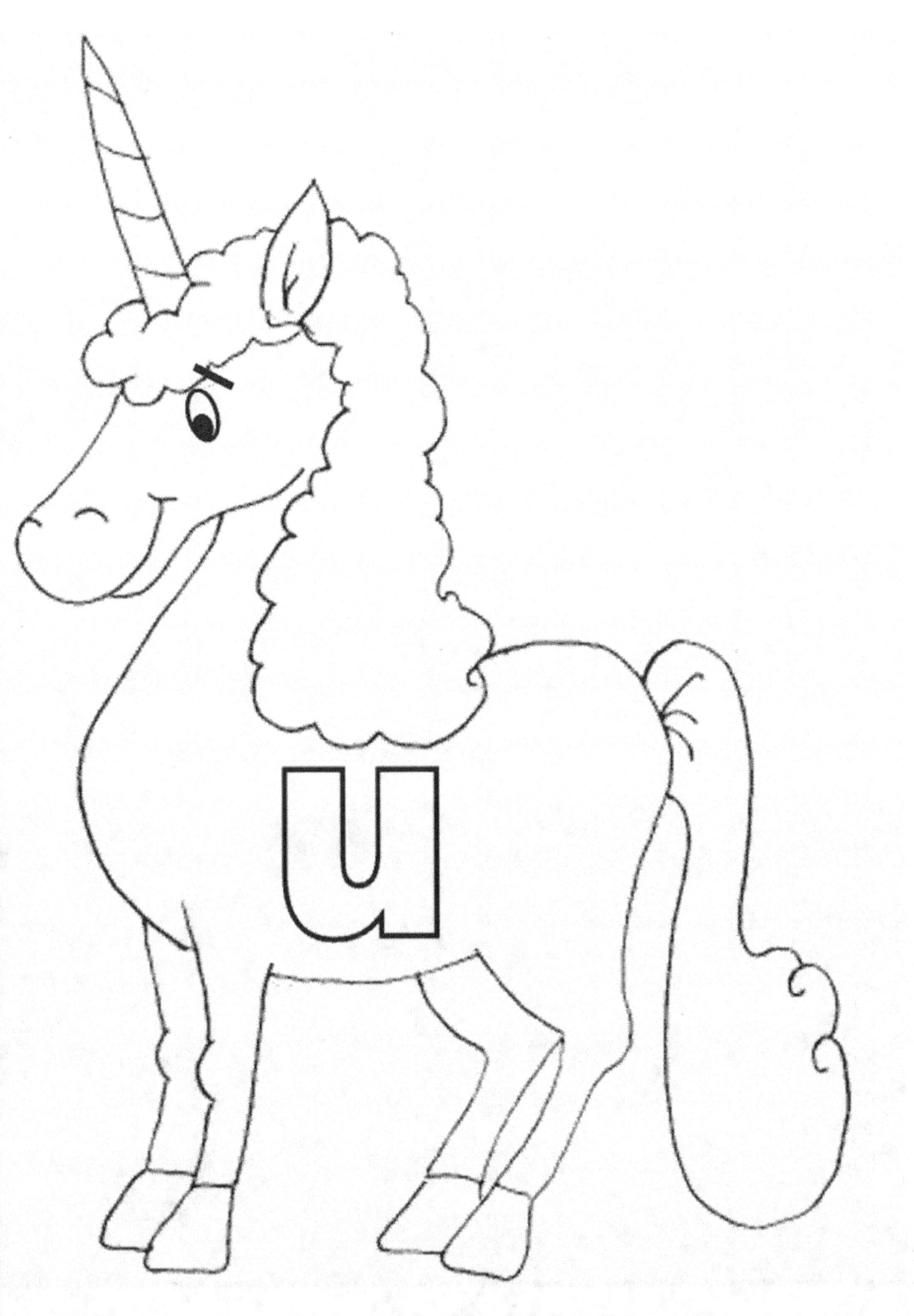

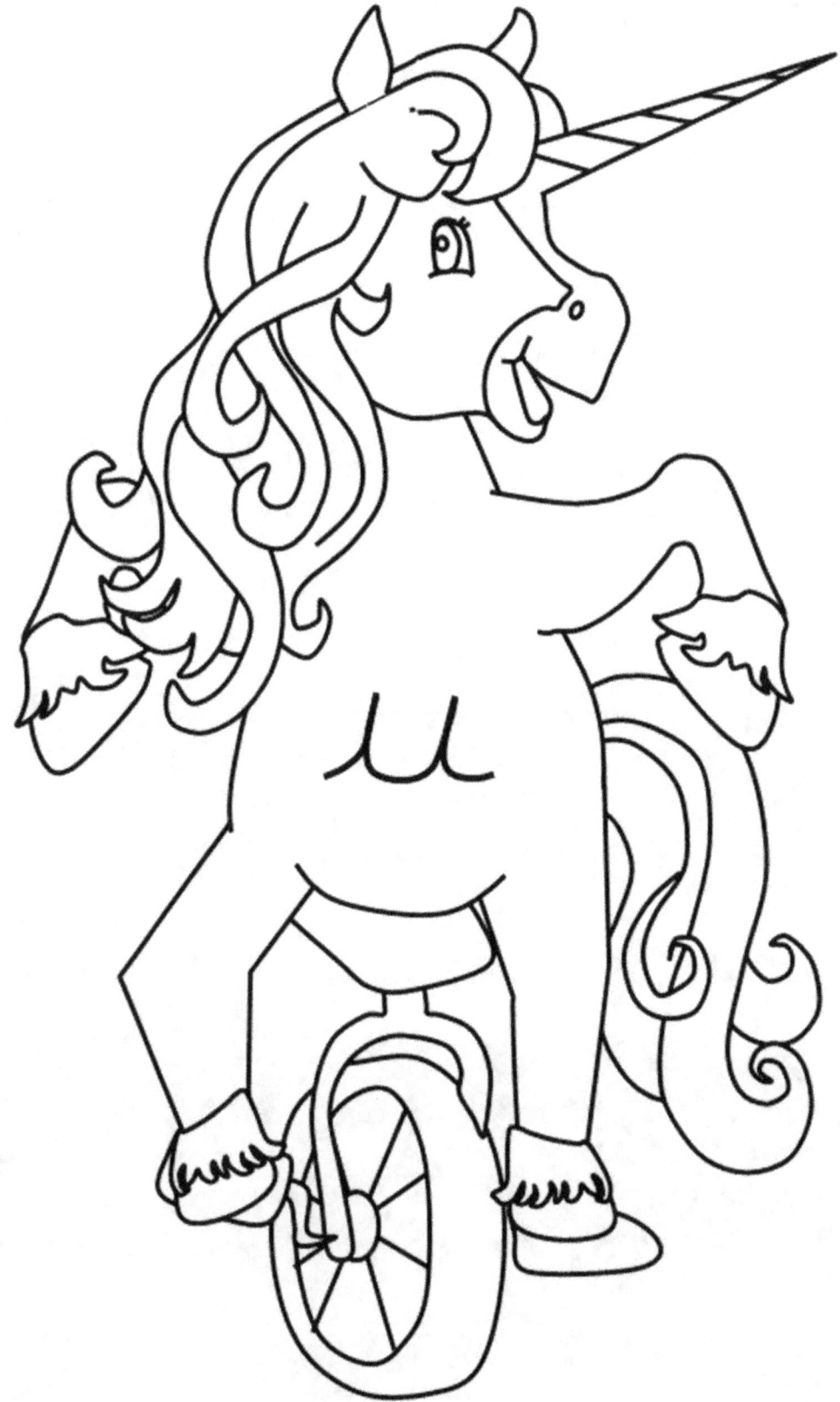

Trace the steps for making the letter u on the following line.

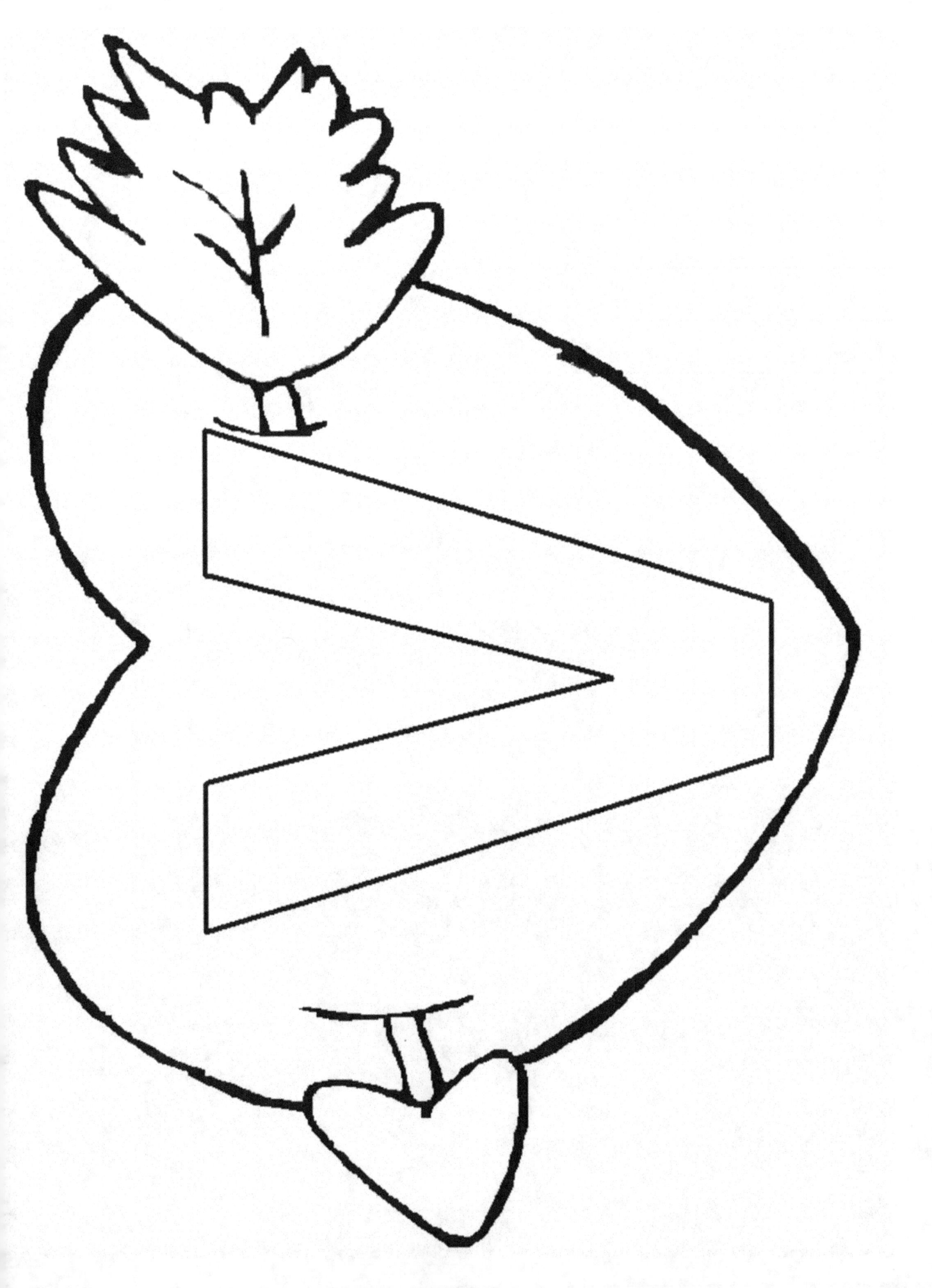

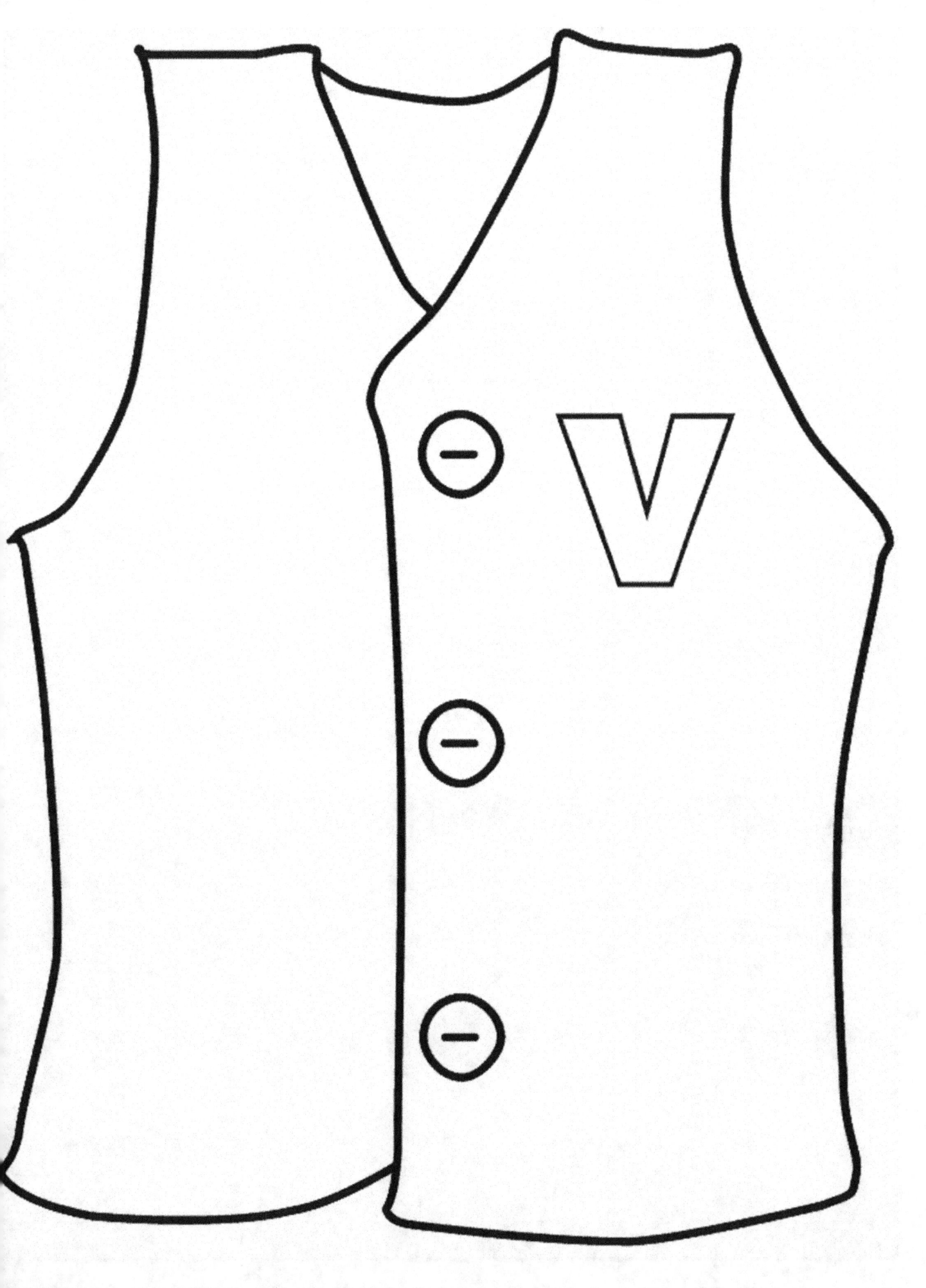

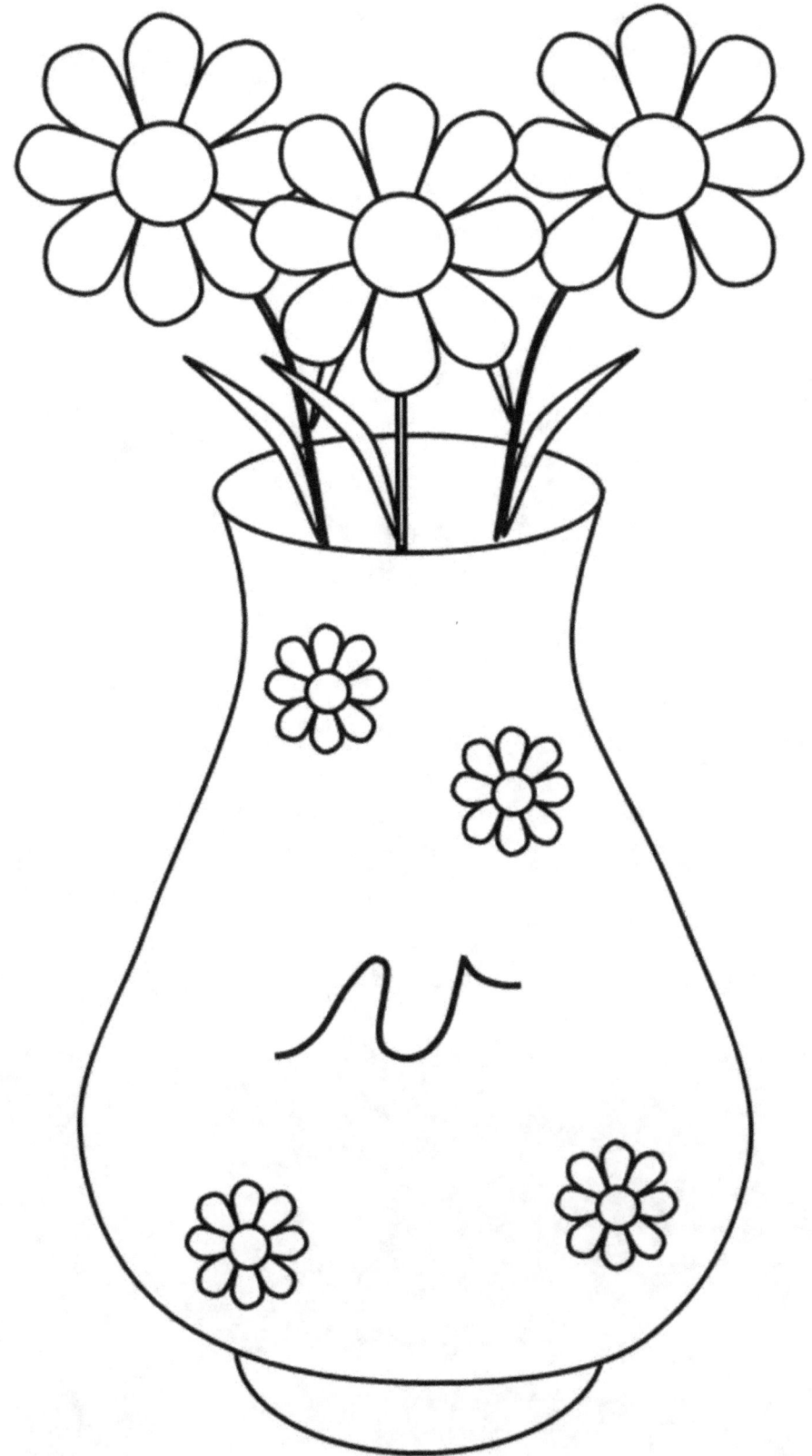

Trace the steps for making the letter v on the following line.

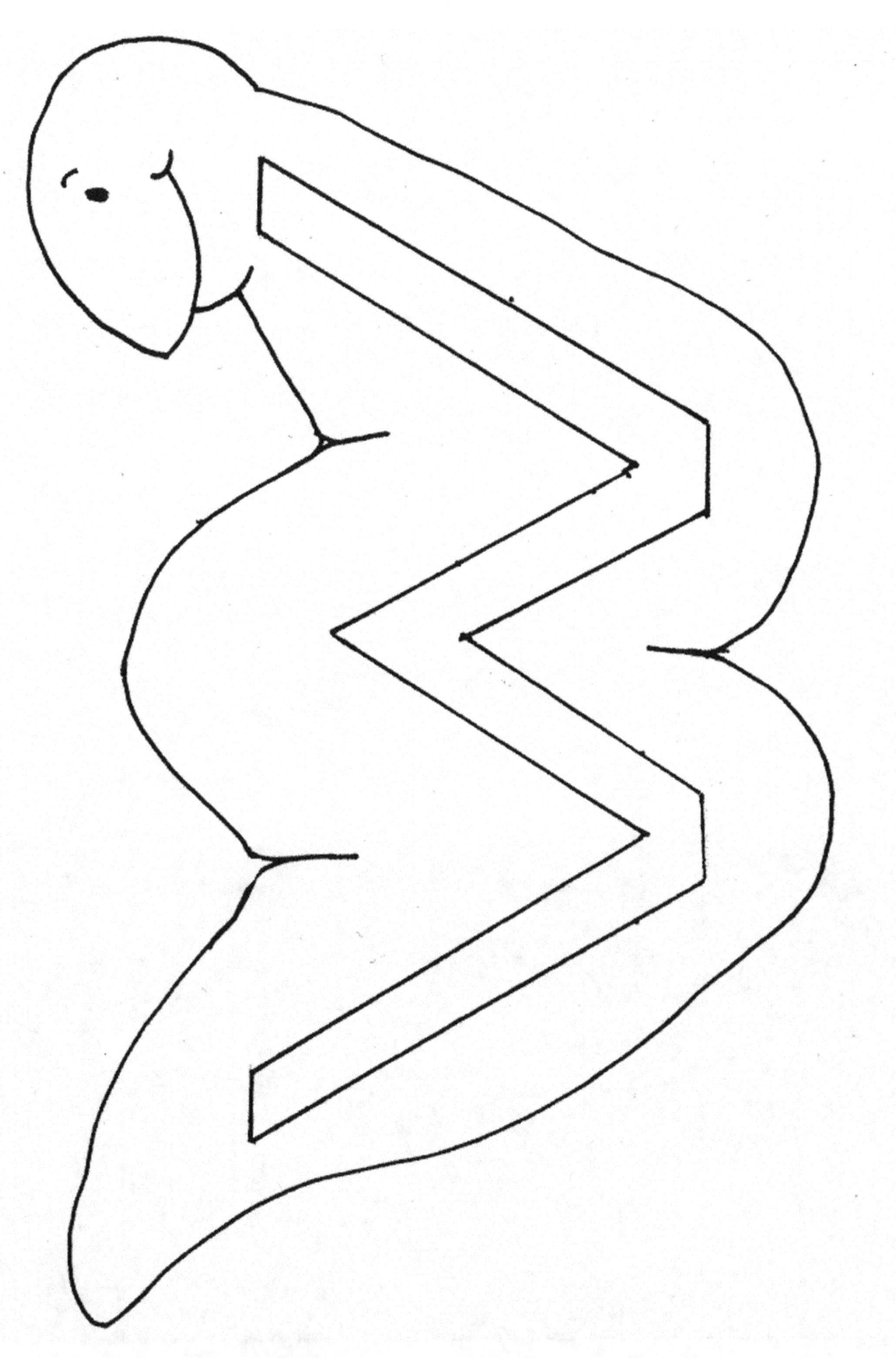

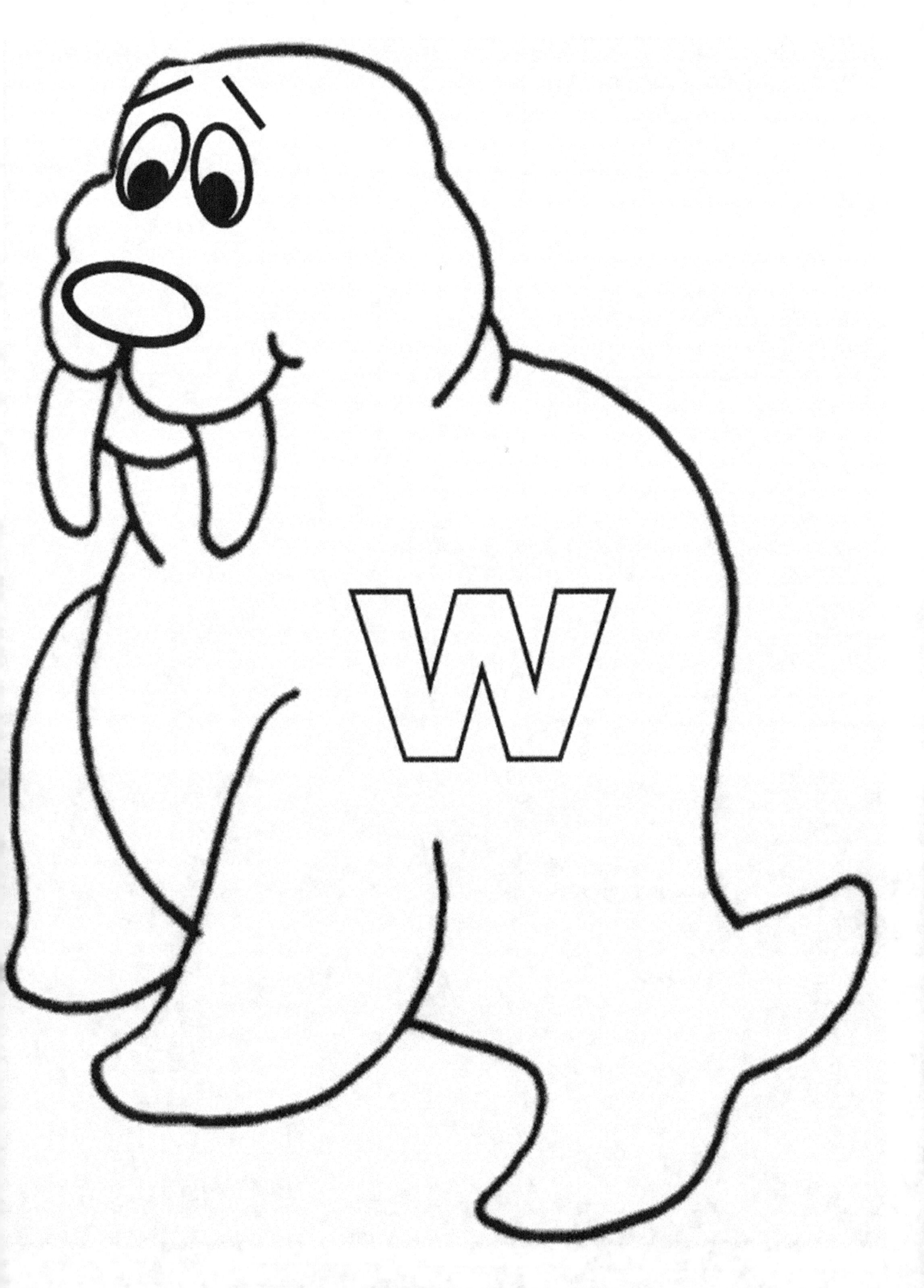

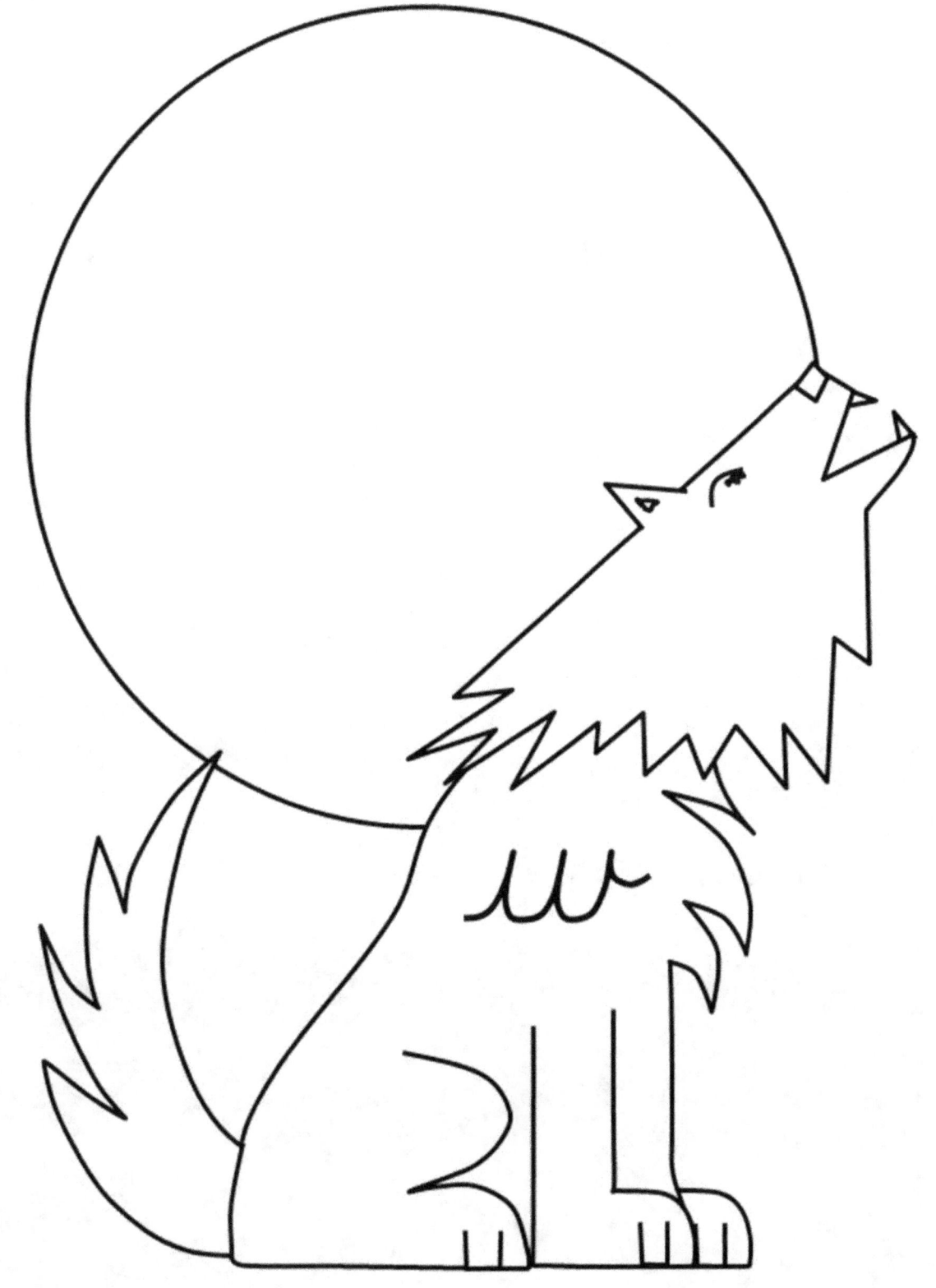

Trace the steps for making the letter w on the following line.

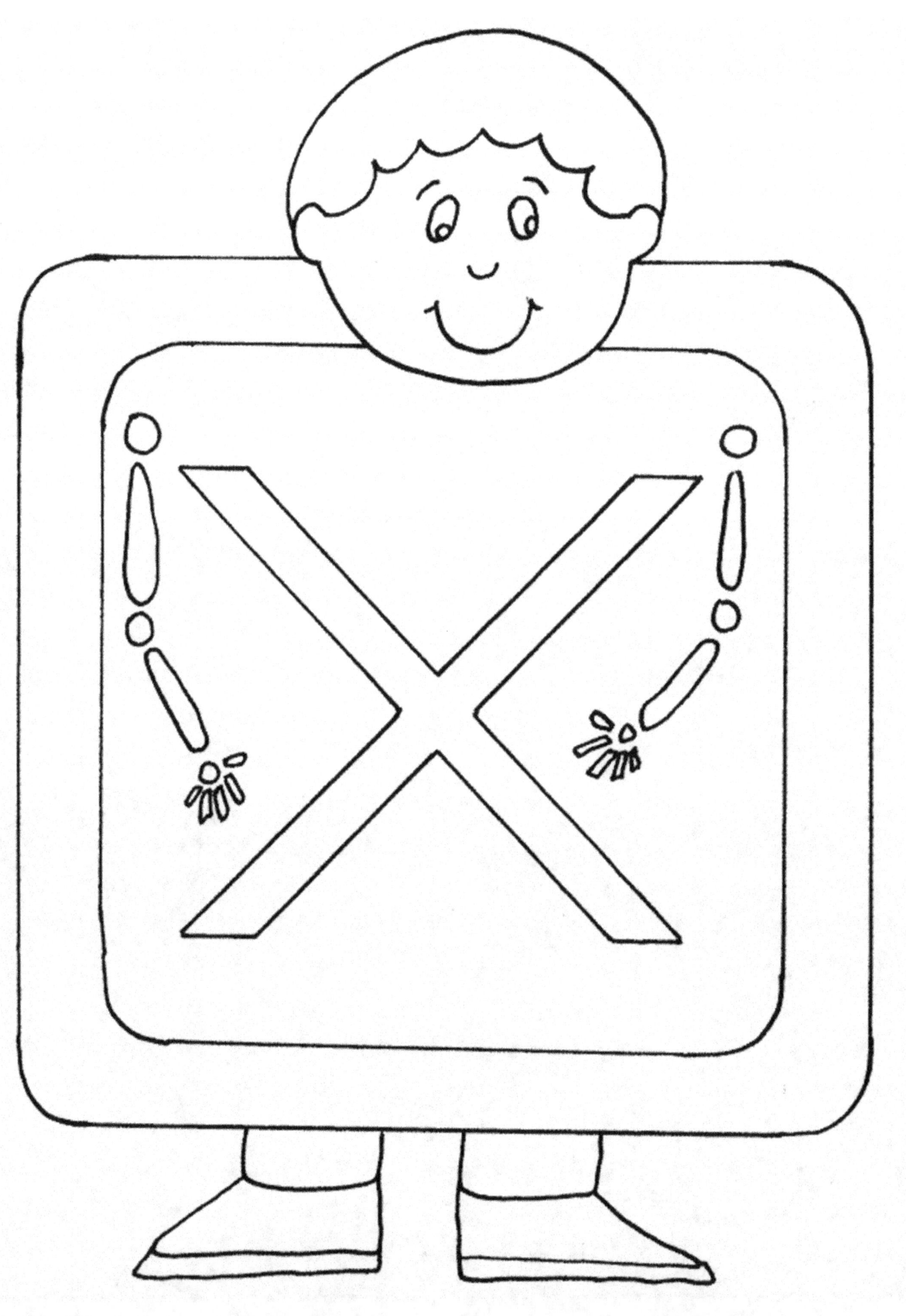

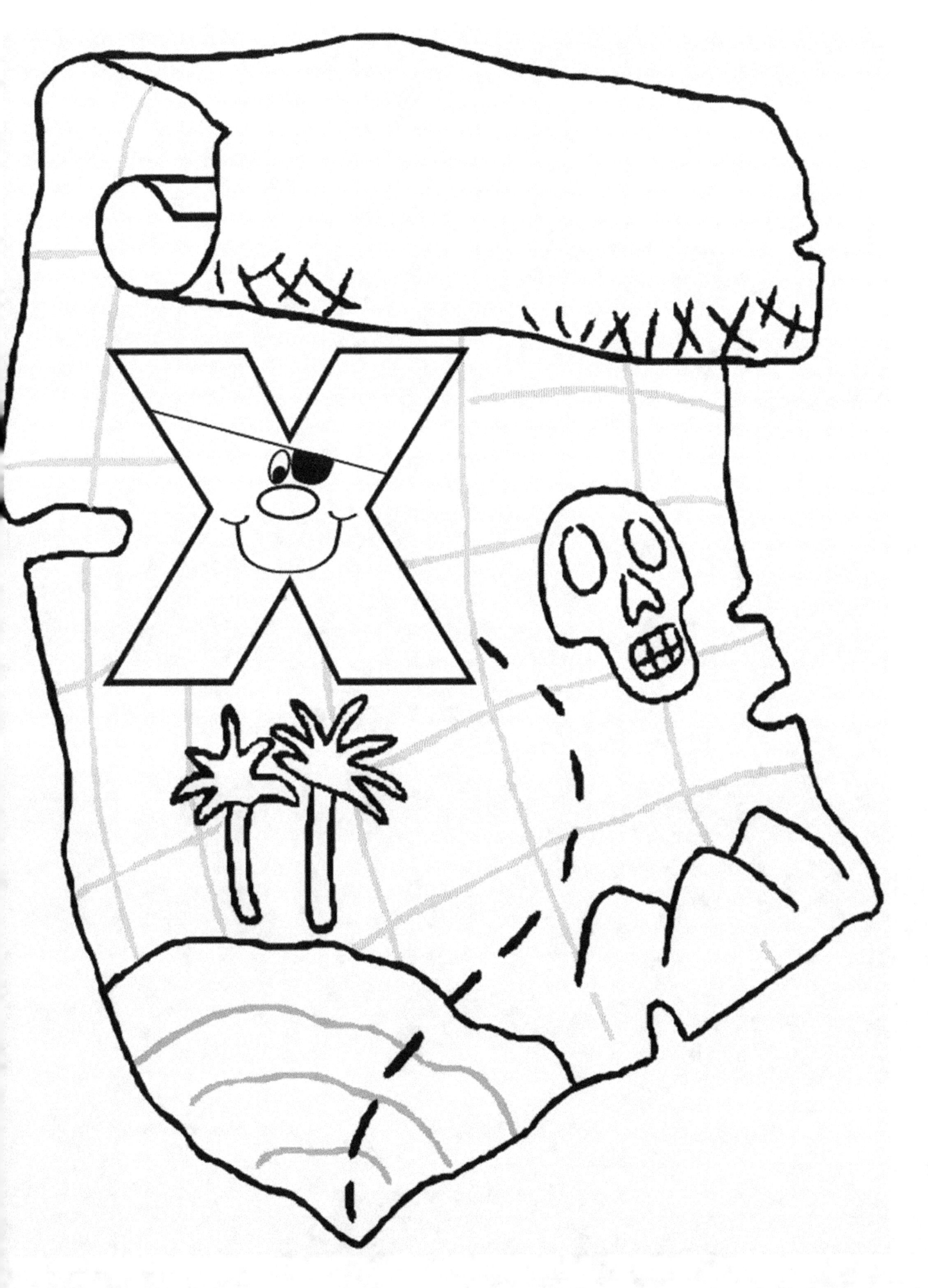

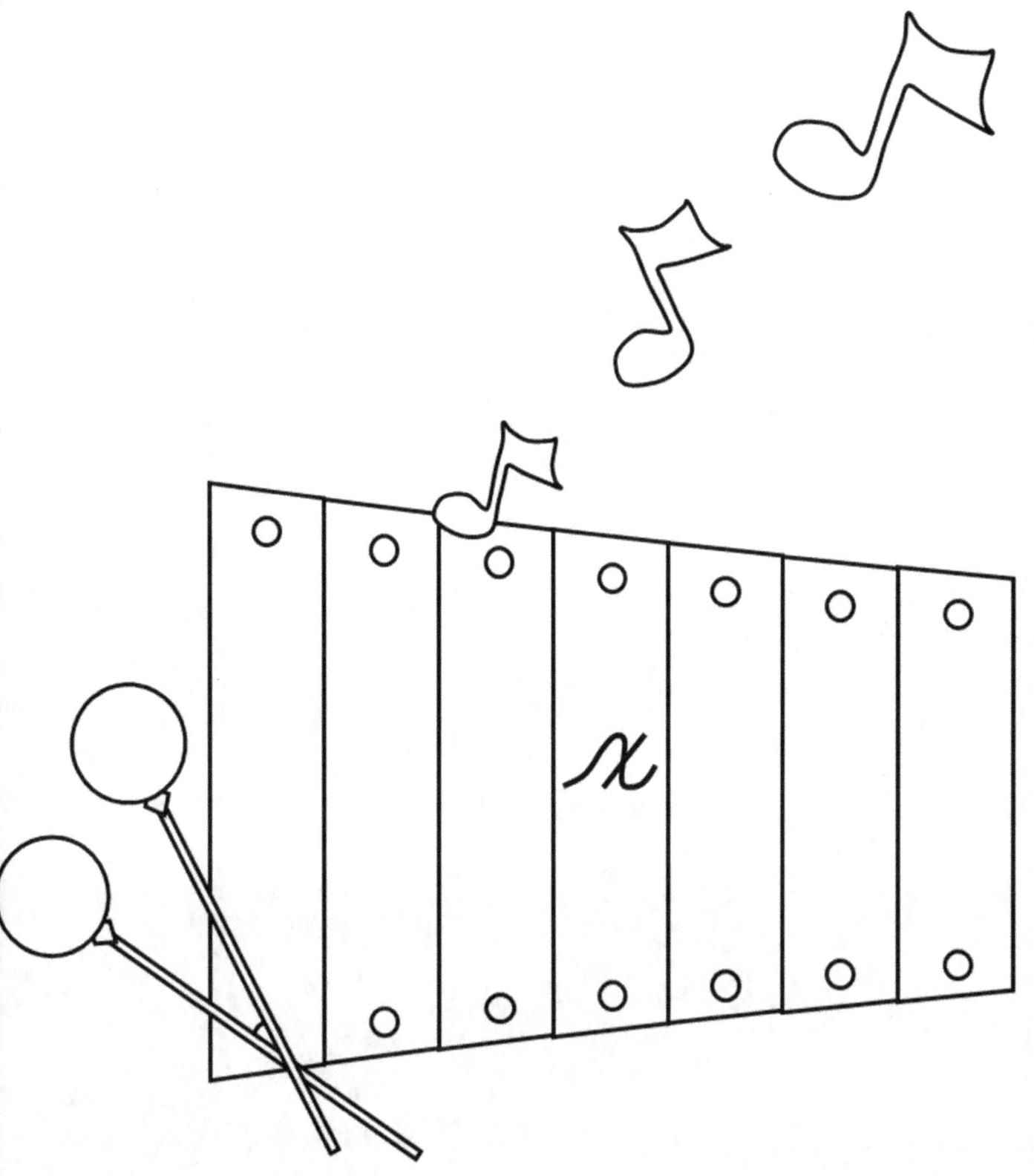

Trace the steps for making the letter x on the following line.

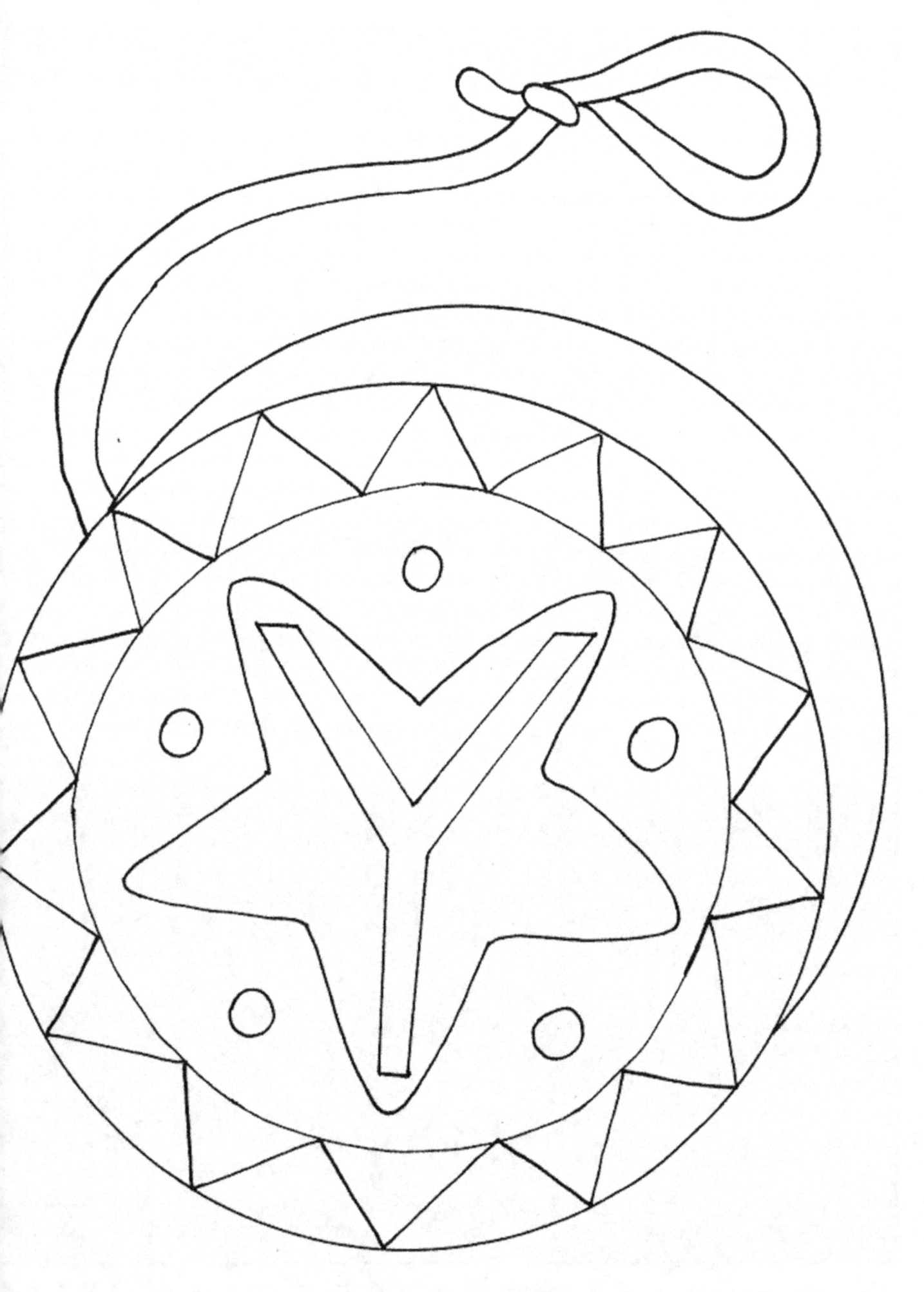

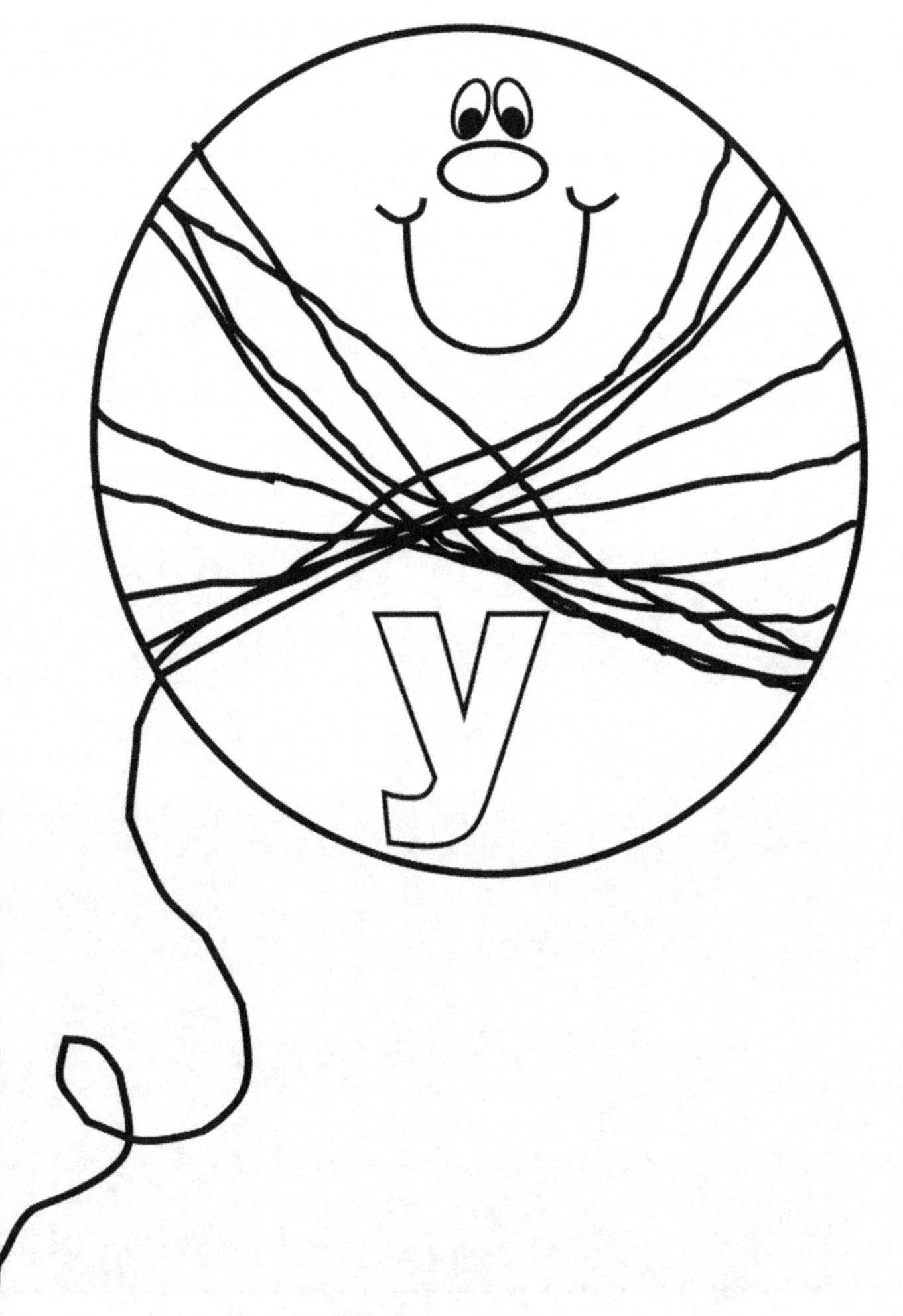

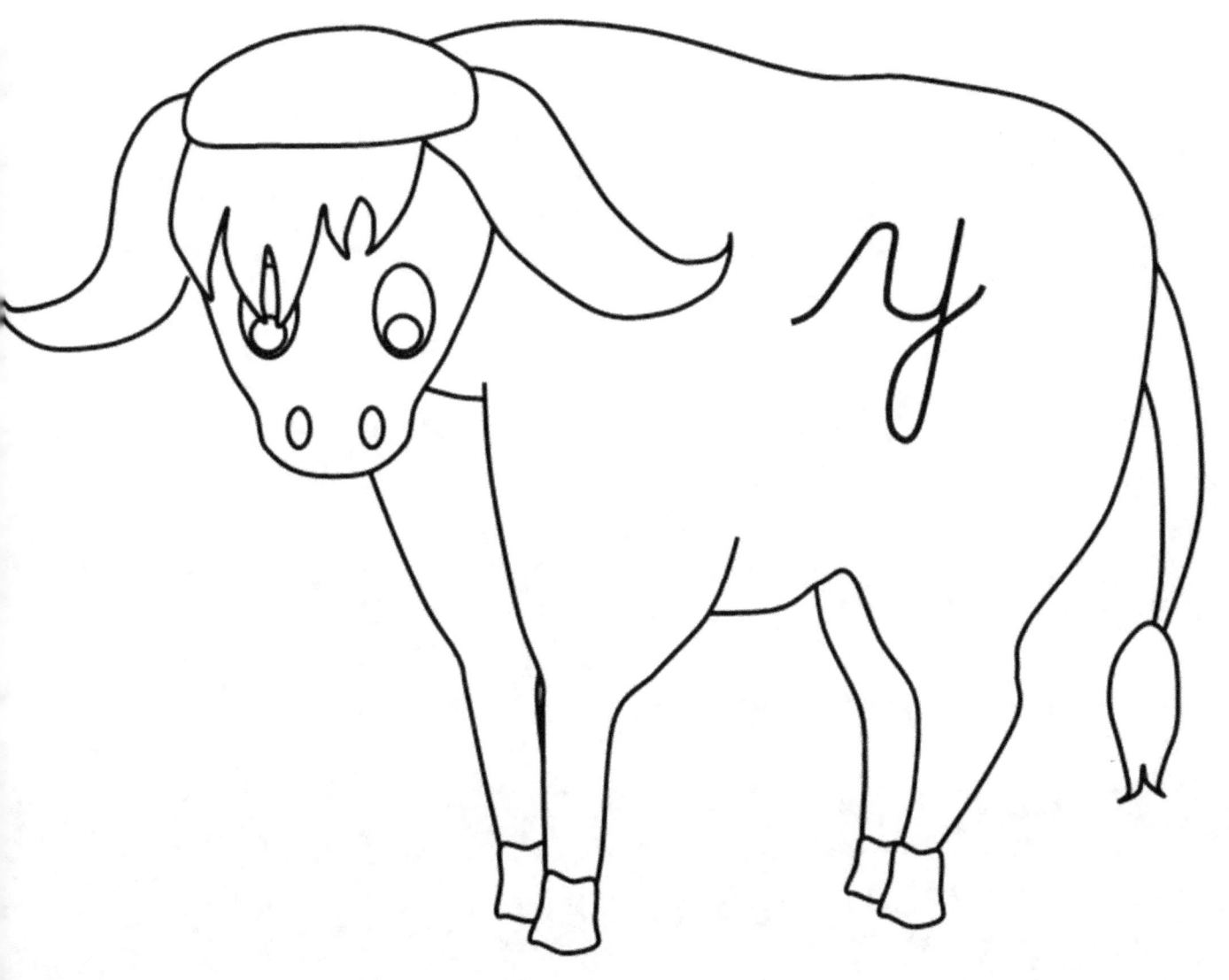

Trace the steps for making the letter y on the following line.

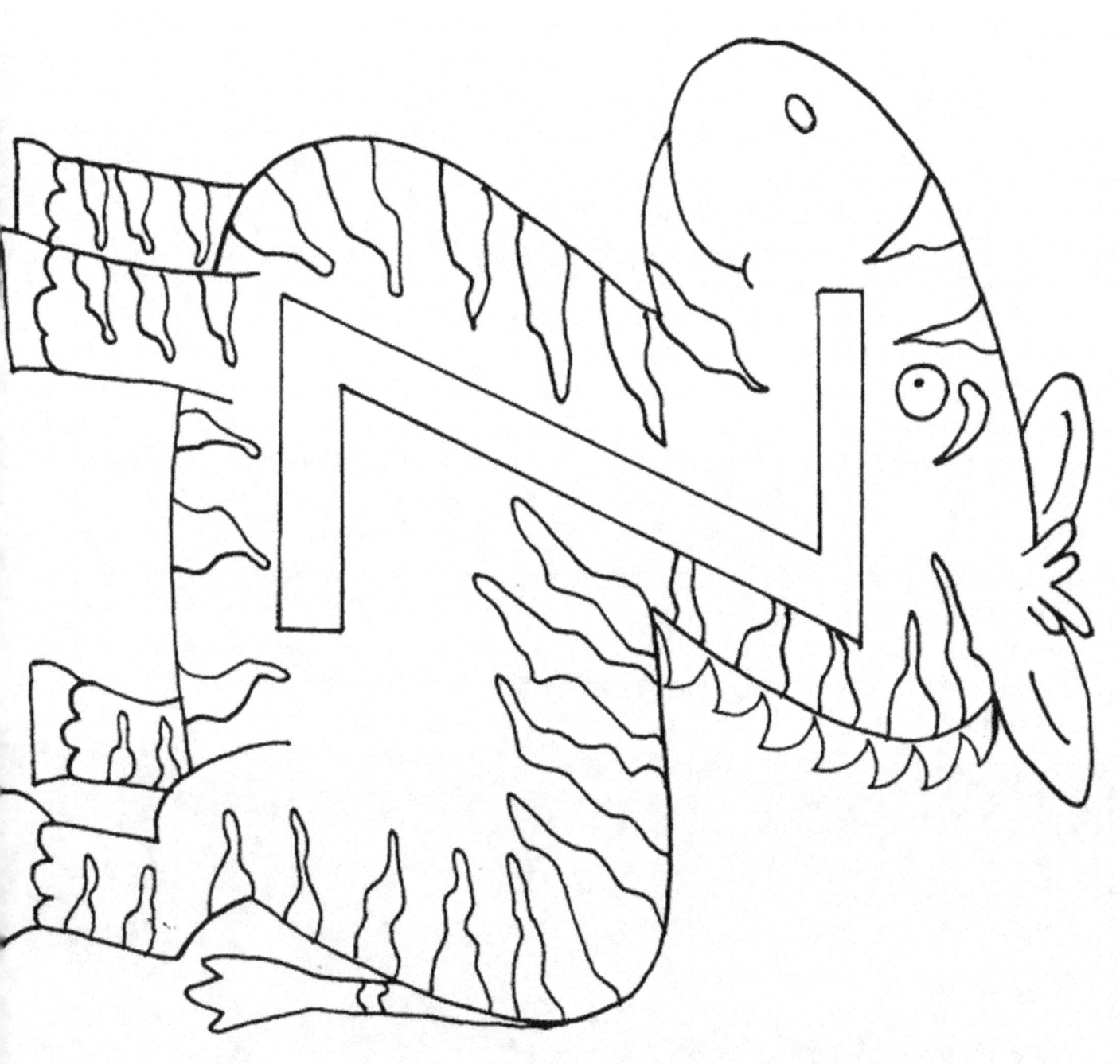

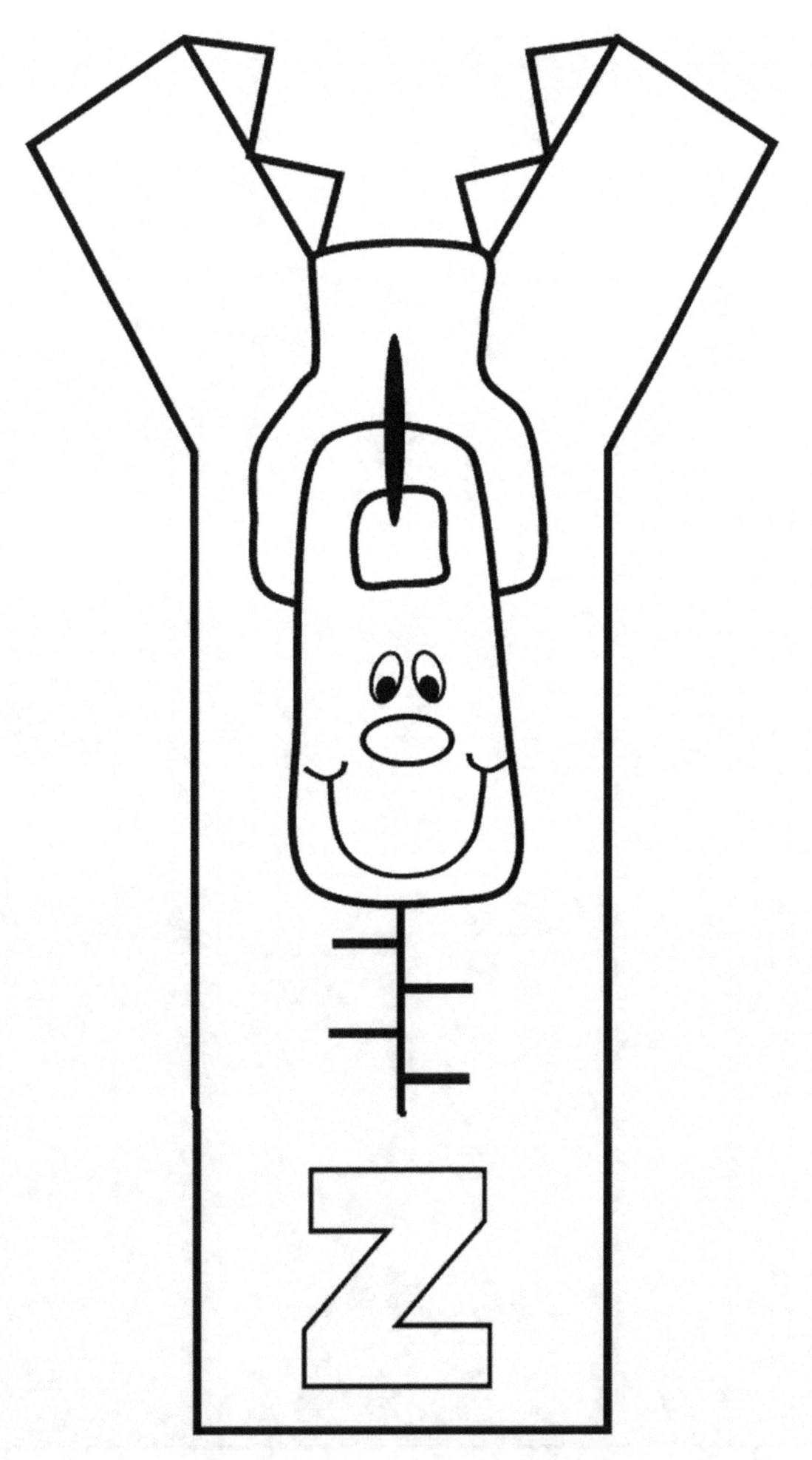

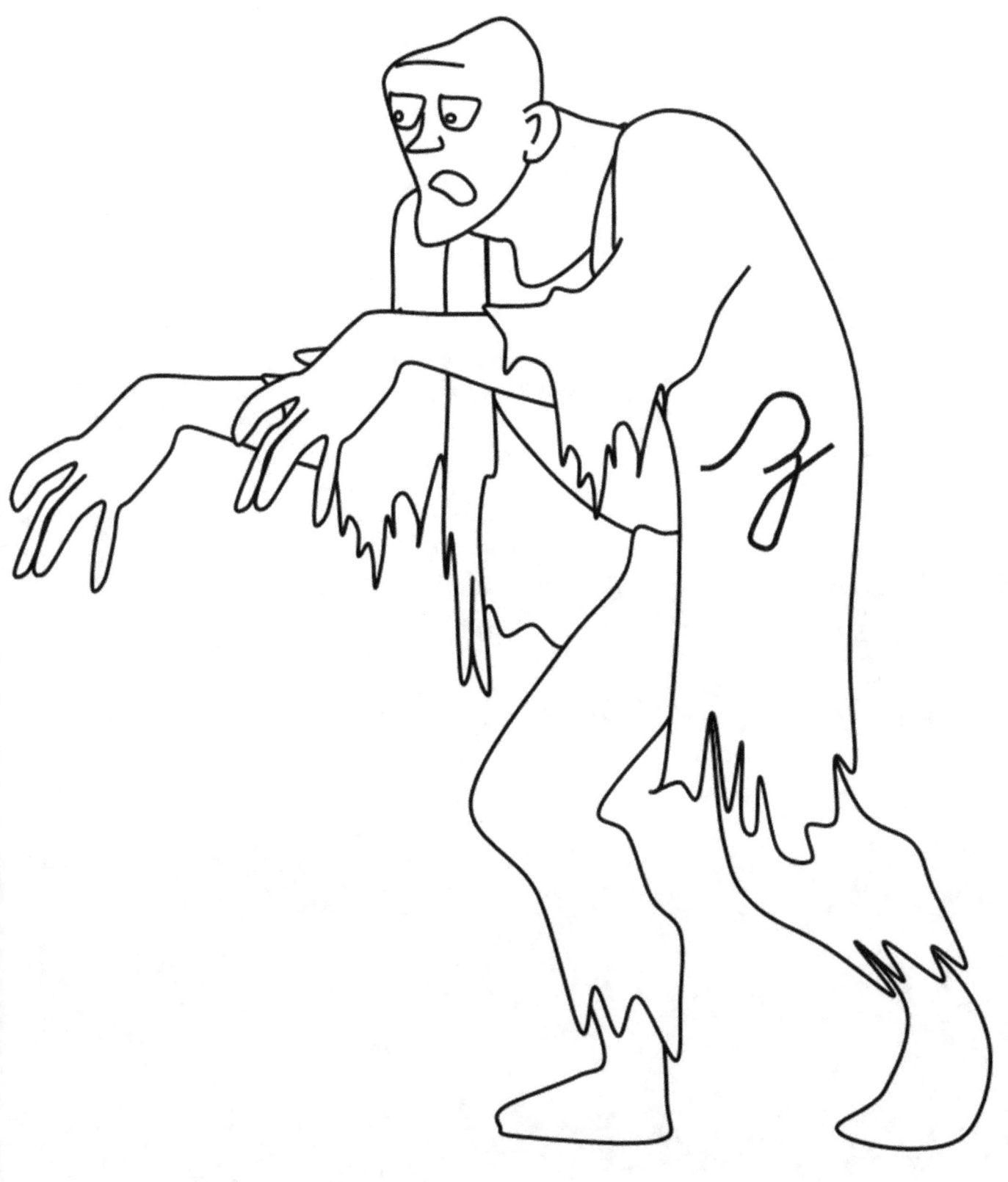

Trace the steps for making the letter z on the following line.

www.ingramcontent.com/pod-product-compliance
Lightning Source LLC
Chambersburg PA
CBHW081512220526
45467CB00010B/2886